TIME TO TAKE FLIGHT

TIME TO TAKE FLIGHT

THE SAVVY WOMAN'S GUIDE TO SAFE SOLO TRAVEL

JAYNE SEAGRAVE

TouchWood
Editions

LIBRARY AND ARCHIVES CANADA CATALOGUING IN PUBLICATION
Seagrave, Jayne, 1961–, author
Time to take flight : the savvy woman's guide to safe solo travel / Jayne Seagrave.

Issued in print and electronic formats.
ISBN 978-1-77151-162-9

1. Middle aged women—Travel—Handbooks, manuals, etc. 2. Older women—
Travel—Handbooks, manuals, etc. 3. Women travelers—Handbooks, manuals, etc.
4. Travel—Safety measures. I. Title.

G465.S42 2016   910.4082   C2015-907630-7

Editor: Renée Layberry
Designer: Pete Kohut
Cover image: Marija Anicic/Stocksy United
Interior illustrations: City silhouettes by Maxger, istockphoto.com except on pages, 154 and 164
(vecteezy.com), 240 (greatvectors.com), 258 (supercoloring.com/silhouettes/edinburgh-skyline)
Travel icons: Lera Efremova, creativemarket.com
Author photo: Elizabeth Hadley

We acknowledge the financial support of the Government of Canada through the Canada Book
Fund and the province of British Columbia through the Book Publishing Tax Credit.

We travel not to escape life, but for life not to escape us.

—Author unknown

Contents

TIME TO TAKE FLIGHT IN EUROPE

FURTHER RESOURCES

GETTING READY
TO TAKE FLIGHT

WHY TAKE A SOLO FLIGHT?

Travel is more than just seeing the sights; it is a change
that goes on, deep and permanent, in the ideas of living.

—Miriam Beard

⟶ **WHEN I WAS EIGHTEEN I** traveled in the USA for the first time
with young man called Rick; I did not know him particularly
well and had met him while working at summer camp. We
arrived in Miami one very hot August day, and I was impatient
to leave our seedy, cheap, poorly furnished motel room and
explore the exciting new city. Rick, however, decided it was
more important to visit the laundry, wash and dry his clothes,
and laboriously organize and color-code his socks. I left him at
the motel and vowed never to travel again with an individual I
did not know *very* well.

This experience has had a long-lasting effect. I believe the best way to travel is the single way, and as I get older this belief only gets stronger. Solo travel is luxurious because you decide the itinerary, travel at your own pace, and see what you want. It's also a challenge, a self-indulgence, and a voyage into self-discovery. Travel broadens the perspective, imparts understanding of other cultures, and makes us real citizens of the world. It opens our eyes, with the real danger being that, upon returning home, the desire to see more is firmly ingrained. For these reasons and more I adore traveling alone and find it totally addictive.

Over the last twenty years, I've spent on average three months out of every year away from home. While almost 50 percent of these excursions have been with my family, the remainder has been for business and traveling to trade shows and conventions in North America and Europe to market tools that my company, the Vancouver Tool Corporation (www .vancouvertool.com), produces for the home improvement industry. I was also heavily involved in a trade association (the Worldwide Do-It-Yourself Council) acting as its president for a couple of years, which required international excursions. I did most of this travel alone. When I mentioned to girlfriends I was off to Guadalajara, Vienna, St. Louis, Rome, or Chicago by myself, many had a wistful look in their eye and commented, "You're so brave!" But I am not brave. In order to grow a business, I have had to travel to seek new markets; by doing so I have learned travel is not scary or difficult for the mature single woman. Confidence and planning are critical; we must beware of limiting ourselves when considering new opportunities in an attempt to justify our actions or non-actions. We all seek the safe option because of ease and a perception that the alternative is threatening, but we secretly yearn for something else.

Solo travel is immensely enjoyable and easily possible, whatever your age, with careful planning. It gives an intense adrenalin rush, which, as we grow older, is more difficult to obtain. Planning and embarking on a new adventure gives me an increased sense of awareness and helps me drop my guard. In my younger days, the opposite sex aroused this kind of excitement, complete with pounding heart, giddy passion, blushing cheeks, heightened awareness, and a preoccupation with the object of my desire. Now, in my fifties, I have these feelings when I arrive in an unfamiliar place. I cannot wait to explore this new home, see the architecture, taste the cuisine, experience the climate, smell the streets, encounter the people, and hear the languages. When I'm away, every sense is more acute, every action more intense. Discovering a new culture and surroundings is like falling in love; knowing the time I have with my new infatuation is limited, I absorb as much as possible and savor each moment of the encounter. Travel is also a way to understand myself, to grow, to contemplate and rejuvenate my life. What's more, solo travel is the perfect time for reflection and reassessment; the focus is just on *you*. In our busy lives there is often not enough time to take stock of where we are and what we want to be; solo travel awards time for this.

I have unapologetically written this book primarily for women over the age of forty who are apprehensive about traveling alone, really want to, and have not done so yet. The existing travel literature barely acknowledges this demographic. My goal is to offer encouragement, advice, and support for these women to fulfill this desire while at the same time providing practical guidance based on first-hand, real-life experiences. My aim is not to replicate the extensive amount of travel literature available in existing guidebooks but rather to supplement this generic information with tips and advice specifically for the solo female traveler. *Time to Take Flight* is a resource to be used alongside the comprehensive site-specific guides available for every North American and European city suitable for the savvy solo girl.

I wrote this book for women who have experienced life changes and are seeking new opportunities. It is not unusual for women who have been married or partnered for many years to find themselves single, divorced, or widowed. Often they'll have a desire to start fresh and change certain elements of their previous lives to adjust to this new state. Travel may be on their agenda, but frequently they have reservations and doubts about how it can be done, or whether they have the confidence to embark on an independent journey. Women who have been busy rearing children who have now left home find themselves with the time and resources to travel, but don't know how to take the first step. These former full-time mothers may be in a happy relationship with a spouse who prefers to stay home and work, or play with their shed/car/garden/tools/TV rather than explore another culture or city. To fulfill independent dreams, these wives need to take flight independently or not go at all. The advice given in the following pages also applies to single women who do not have a friend or spouse with whom they can confidently travel—and it's advice that will work for those who, like me, dread organized group holidays and dislike being among strangers and their own idiosyncrasies with no safe haven to escape to. I pepper the text with personal anecdotes to illustrate the unique, often humorous memories created when traveling as a solo woman. Admittedly, every venture—whether alone or with company—provides opportunities for such memories, but when you're going solo they are unique to you, cannot be challenged or reinterpreted by others, and exist for you to savor for years to come.

I believe what stops most women from traveling alone is not the logistics of money, time, employment, or commitments, but rather a lack of confidence. Embarking on an excursion alone seems frightening, and it's easy for us to feel nervous about a proposed venture. Many women feel they will be the object of pity from friends or couples who perceive them as "lonely old dears" without any friends. In truth, many of these people will be envious of your independence.

—→ BENEFITS

In 2015, a travel advisory survey of over nine thousand women in seven countries found that 74 percent of women planned to travel solo that year—an increase from 41 percent who had previous experience traveling alone. So why are so many women doing it or planning to do it? Probably because of the benefits identified with travel, most notably relaxation and rejuvenation. A number of websites offer extensive advice to parents over how to reduce stress when traveling with your family and particularly with children, indicating that these vacations, in contrast to ones taken alone, are anything but stress free.

I love my husband and teenage sons—I truly do (well, *most* of the time)—but I can recount numerous family vacations that were anything but relaxed. While holidaying with my family I've had bizarre, unforgettable, stress-filled incidents that pulled me toward the realization that solo travel is the far calmer alternative. I recall my offspring needing numerous stitches for head injuries received at 3 AM in the Australian outback; holding my two-year-old in my arms as he projectile vomited over the well-dressed, single, male German tourist sitting next to us during the first hour of an eight-hour transatlantic flight; and so many loud, emotional, and frequently violent sibling arguments over issues as important as who uses the ketchup first, or sits behind the driver in the car, or selects the next CD for everyone's entertainment—all issues worthy of intervention by the United Nations, clearly. Yes, Middle East conflict is nothing compared to my two sons' arguments while on holiday and the failed diplomatic attempts of their parents. Is it any wonder I'm an advocate for solo travel? Such stresses do not happen when alone.

Some of the benefits of traveling alone are increased confidence, greater cultural understanding, education, broadened horizons and perspectives, and a new sense of adventure. Travel is a real form of empowerment and is easier and more affordable than ever in the twenty-first century. It does not have to involve long, exotic trips to sun-drenched beaches on faraway islands; it can simply be a night away to a city only a few hours from home.

The benefits of traveling alone frequently outweigh those of traveling with others. When alone, I can get up when I want, and I can eat what, when, and where I want. I can visit the places I want to see and leave when I've had enough. I do not have to accommodate anyone else—the only timetable is my own. I can be totally selfish when single; solo travel is utterly self-indulgent. When traveling with others, so much time is spent focusing on them because it is polite to do so. But being alone grants the power to regulate your own life. Ernest Hemingway put it succinctly when he said, "Never go on a trip with anyone you do not love."

While lifelong spouses and best friends may tick all the required camaraderie boxes, if they do not deliver on the travel one I believe it is in everyone's interest to leave them at home with the dog, cumbersome luggage, and inflatable pillows. As a young woman I spent one memorable summer during my undergraduate studies fantasizing about trekking around Europe with a tall, incredibly good-looking, cricket-obsessed, fit creature I was infatuated with but who hardly noticed me. I saw nothing wrong with wanting to explore new countries by day and his body by night—an ambition I failed to fully articulate and, consequently, one he failed to recognize. I now realize, had he come to his senses, identified my passion, and delivered on these fantasies, a lot of tears and money would have been wasted, probably before we obtained the foreign currency.

Dreaming of travel destinations is a legitimate and worthy activity that takes time; traveling with another being is a momentous task and takes not only a huge amount of time but also a colossal amount of courage. At age twenty I was naïve in my travel (and romantic) ambitions; as we get older the selfish gene takes over, and we become set in our ways—another reason for solo flight. While I may have been able to accommodate my Adonis in younger days (albeit for the short term on a predominantly physical level), I wouldn't be willing to accommodate him now, even if he showed up looking like Richard Gere. My sensible gene would inevitably come into play, and besides, I need to take flight alone to ensure I enjoy to the fullest extent my selfish sojourn.

Ever since I can remember, all my spare money has been spent on travel and on gaining experiences, not material possessions. In my late teens and early twenties, my girlfriends invested in expensive French skin creams, designer clothes, numerous cocktails, cars, and, of course, shoes while I saved for my next trip. When I look in the mirror or compare my wrinkly features with those of my high school cohort, I have a fleeting twinge of regret that a few of these travel dollars were not allocated all those years ago to anti-aging skin creams, but if given the opportunity again I would not alter my purchasing choices. My energy and enthusiasm for new countries and cultures lives on forty years later and is ageless. *Je ne regrette rein.*

I hope the suggestions in the following pages will kick-start those who have been procrastinating for years and will act as a boot camp to encourage change and action. As we grow older, many parts of our bodies do not function in the way they used to—long strenuous hikes are out, more trips to the restroom are in, and it takes longer to recover from bouts of flu or pulled muscles. We never know what's around the next corner, so we should acknowledge the benefits travel creates and act today.

⟶ GETTING OVER THE EXCUSES

I thought of writing this book for about five years before I approached a publisher with an actual proposal. During that time I had been listening to women wistfully acknowledge they would like to travel alone, but for a multitude of reasons could not, or so they thought. In my experience, women tend to come up with a whole bunch of excuses for not traveling. They might be reluctant to leave their family, they may fear dining alone, or think they do not have the money or time. All these barriers are real, but by acknowledging them they can be addressed, understood, and accepted.

Family Commitments

Many women feel guilty leaving children and spouses alone and for this reason decide not to travel. However, I firmly believe solo travel by wives and mothers is good for family relationships. Too often women become trapped within the roles of mother, spouse, daughter, wife, and friend, with little time to stand back and relate to oneself as an individual. Solo travel grants the opportunity to do this. I left my four-month-old son for ten days, having to free him from the breast to do so. My two boys are now teenagers and do not appear to have been damaged by their mother's (and father's) absences during their formative years, although they would undoubtedly challenge this claim, citing their inability to conjugate French verbs and get beyond level five in swimming lessons, along with their inadequate understanding of the minds of teenage girls.

I *love* it when my spouse travels and leaves me alone with the kids. We develop a unique rapport and enjoy mother/sons bonding by doing things Dad would not approve of (evenings spent watching back-to-back episodes of *Big Bang Theory* on TV, having cold pizza for breakfast, singing loudly to Katy Perry in the car with the windows down, irrespective of the season). Likewise, I know the boys love it when I leave and the nagging stops. You may feel indispensable in the household; well, get over yourself—you are not. Okay, sure, upon your return you will probably unearth a mountain of unwashed, smelly clothes; discover green, unidentifiable, rank food growing bacteria in the back of the fridge; and maybe find goldfish/plants/maiden aunts have died without anyone noticing. But your family will have survived and probably thrived. And, on a positive note, you will have been missed and therefore more appreciated upon return (although in my experience this emotion quickly erodes).

You can, of course, address the stress of leaving a spouse and children by filling the freezer with food, leaving copious pages of instructions (which will probably be ignored and only serve the purpose of making the author feel better) and telling family friends and neighbors you will be away. Obviously the age (and work commitments) of the spouse and/or children will influence decisions about travel destinations and length of trip, but whatever their ages, four days away is not a long time, will not kill them, and may be the break everyone needs. The barrier to travel is frequently the woman herself; to overcome this, imagine how refreshed and content you'll feel following the trip, and remind yourself that it's deserved. If it's your first solo excursion, seek the family's support and encouragement.

Now for a real confession: I love being away from my family, and when abroad I rarely miss them. When traveling, I'm often asked if I think of my kids; this is when I blush and stutter as I try to recall if I do actually have children and what their names are. For the most part I'm too busy to consider them; then I feel guilty. When discussing this with other women who have also left significant others at home, I find it to be a common sentiment (as is the guilt we feel over not thinking about them when asked if we are). However, to alleviate any such guilt, remind yourself that if you already have a strong relationship with your spouse and children, leaving them for a short period of time will only strengthen your ties.

Many long-established couples acknowledge that as they

grow older, interests diversify. My spouse has ambitions to take long, sweaty, Lycra-clad cycling excursions in Third World countries not known for their sanitation and trips to cold climates to see soccer games. I share neither of these passions, but I still encourage him to participate; we should not deny each other our respective dreams. An American Express travel survey recently recognized the growth of spouse-free holidays taken by individuals in stable, secure marriages who recognize they have divergent aims. Far from being an indication of a failing marriage, these trips can act to strengthen relationships. Encouraging a spouse to travel is not only good for the one striking out on the adventure—it's also good for the well-being of the one left behind. With your partner away, time alone in your own environment can be celebrated.

When my spouse leaves me, I'm free to please myself without having to worry about someone else's needs and expectations. I can, for example, go to bed at 7 PM with copious amounts of fizzy white wine, family-size bags of white cheddar popcorn, and the best classic romantic film ever made, *Brief Encounter*, which I indulge in at least twice a year, always in my husband's absence. Unfettered and on my own, this red-eyed, semi-drunk mess can fall asleep among the popcorn kernels without any shame—such bliss!

There is also the added benefit of having one partner caring for the house/plants/animals/relations while the other is away. Upon return, new stories and experiences can be shared, maybe adding a spark to what has become a stayed relationship—a win-win scenario. How many failing or unfulfilled marriages could be saved if only those in these relationships took time to travel alone?

Loneliness

Another frequently cited barrier to solo travel is loneliness. While there will inevitably be times when you yearn for company, if you plan your holiday well and pack it full of activities, you can keep these emotions at bay. Traveling alone often means more interaction with others; people talk to the single individual more readily than to a couple. Exhausting yourself during the day with a tight agenda of visits to museums, galleries, tours, walking, exploring, and getting lost ensures little time to regret being by yourself. Taking a bus, boat, or walking tour in a new city necessitates the involvement of others. At the very least, listening to an audio narrative means the mind is focused on learning about the holiday destination, not upon being alone. Opting to stay in small bed-and-breakfast-type accommodations and not large hotels will lead to more face-to-face encounters, so you should consider this arrangement if being sociable is on the agenda or a special concern for you. Alternatively, booking a hotel with fitness center, pool, and hot tub necessitates encountering and socializing with individuals using these facilities.

I recently spent a night in Glasgow and met three wonderful, heavy-set women in the small, overheated hotel swimming pool. None of these girls (who were similar in age to me) made any attempt at swimming; instead they moved their arms through the water while standing in the shallow end gossiping and laughing loudly. There were only four of us in the water, and after completing a few lengths I paused and was quickly invited into their conversation, which centered on the merits of large formal weddings, the best way to remove tight, body-shaping underwear, and finding a decent plumber for "little jobs."

(This last topic spawned a great deal of laughter and quips made in a thick Scottish accent, which I did not always comprehend.) It soon became apparent they were keen on avoiding any physical exercise; their time in the pool was meant for weekly socializing, not physical exertion. I spent an hour in the pool but swam very few lengths, and retired to my room with all social needs met, along with a cache of new, wonderful memories. Exercise can happen at any time, but entertaining counsel from Glaswegian women is rare. I doubt I would have met them if traveling with a companion.

Fill up the day and return to your accommodations tired and ready to drop into bed with a glass (or bottle) of wine and BBC World Service or CNN (often the only English-language TV channels available in some European countries); you won't have time to think about being alone. I rarely take long bubble baths at home, but after a strenuous day of walking around a new city, a glass of wine in the bath can be the perfect tonic. (By the way, tubs in Europe are larger and deeper than in North America, adding to this luxury.) Another way to fill up your day and curb any potential loneliness is to take in theater and shows, either in the afternoon or evening, easily accessible in larger cities (e.g., London, Las Vegas, Chicago, New York). Relatively diminutive destinations can hold surprising options too, if you look for them. While staying in the small Scottish town of Oban, I discovered a community cinema seating only fifteen; everyone in the audience spoke to one another, so it felt like watching TV in a friend's living room rather than in a commercial space. Bottom line: make the most of new surroundings and fill up time—it will mean you're too busy to be reflective.

Only on longer trips (more than ten days away) do I start

to miss my home and family and think about returning home. When feeling lonely, the urge to call home is most acute. Try to resist this; it can make you feel worse once the call ends. It's much better to make contact when things are going well.

In summary, my recommendations for getting over feelings of loneliness is to take public transit, go on a walking tour, write in a journal, read an enthralling book, send emails and postcards, or sit in the bar of a large hotel and people watch. During these bar times, your gaze will inevitably be drawn to the dour-looking married couple nursing their drinks, staring in different directions, playing with their cell phones without engaging each other in conversation or making eye contact. When I encounter these duos (and I see them everywhere), I wonder who is lonelier—them or me?

Dining Alone

I've often heard women express the fear of dining alone as a barrier to solo travel. And I can identify. We all have this misguided idea everyone is looking at us; we feel conspicuous, but in truth, those around us are not interested in the fifty-year-old broad with her highlighted hair and sensible shoes, eating alone. People are too concerned with their own little worlds to consider us. Remember this truth when nervous about anything.

I was a very, very shy child until the age of twelve; then I became a very, very loud teenager, a trait that's remained with me. This change of character can be attributed to two things: First, as a child, I believed God had allocated me a pre-determined number of words (don't laugh!) and that when these were spent I would die; it took until puberty to realize this belief was misguided and that he was actually not interested in what I did and did not say. Since that time, as many can attest, I have been making up for this flawed belief and subsequently have trouble remaining quiet. Second, toward the end of elementary school, I was asked a question by a teacher and gave the wrong answer. Acutely embarrassed, I dwelt on it at length but then realized the rest of the class soon forgot about it and moved on. No one noticed me that day in the classroom; my classmates had their own issues to contend with. In exactly the same way forty years later, no one notices when I enter a restaurant and sit down to eat by myself. If God and my elementary school classmates were not interested in me, neither are hungry individuals in foreign restaurants.

When traveling by myself I do not dine out at night in nice restaurants; I do that when I'm traveling with my spouse and family, or when I'm at home, or when I'm on a business trip with colleagues. When alone in a new city I always eat a good breakfast by myself in the hotel's dining room or at an adjacent coffee bar/restaurant (if the hotel does not have a dining room there is usually one nearby). I use this early part of the day to plan an itinerary, reacquaint myself with maps, change the agenda if the weather is not cooperating, and steal an apple from the buffet for later. Breakfast is not my main meal of the day when I'm at home, but when traveling it is. I fill up on the buffet, return to my room for bathroom commitments, and leave prepared for the day.

In a new place, I tend to snack on the cuisine the city or country is famous for (food trucks in Portland, French fries in Amsterdam, gelato in Rome, gateaux in Vienna, goulash in Prague); this usually involves researching numerous casual eating establishments. These stops provide an opportunity to rest tired feet, reread travel guides, peruse literature collected from tourist information centers, write emails, and plan the next few hours. Eating alone is great for people watching, which can help you get over any feelings of embarrassment. Keep occupied with reading material or email and accept the fact that no one is looking at you.

At the end of the day, I return to my accommodations exhausted and purchase wine or beer—along with cheese, salads, fruit, and anything else that appeals to me—from a nearby establishment, usually identified earlier that morning. I put on pajamas, collect towels from the bathroom, and lay them on my bed for my picnic; I eat and drink in this location because an indulgence of this sort is not awarded at home. In the last ten years, a number of supermarkets across the globe (e.g., Tesco Express in the UK, Europe, and Asia; Marks and Spencer in many European cities; other large supermarket chains in the USA) have developed great takeout deli counters. These offer choices that are perfect for eating in a hotel room. With this in mind, I pack Starbucks instant coffee sachets, as well as a corkscrew, bottle opener, and plastic knife, fork, and spoon. I also occasionally use room service, but beware: surcharges for food delivery can be high, so remember to read the small print—otherwise, a tasty fifteen-dollar salad can become thirty dollars' worth of avoidable regret.

At other times I end up wandering into shops and revise any plans to return to my hotel by 7 PM. This is more likely to happen during the summer months when dinner can consist of a gelato on the street while mingling with other tourists, or stopping at an Internet café to send emails while I have a snack. With only yourself to consider and no one monitoring the caloric amount and required food groups of your chosen diet, the dining possibilities for the single dame are endless.

If you're significantly nervous about dining alone, you can always practice before leaving your hometown. Take yourself out for a solo dinner date to a hotel restaurant or bar; consider being seated at the bar itself—it's less conspicuous than sitting at a table for two in the middle of the restaurant, and can be quite pleasant and sociable. Then try your newly acquired skills at eating establishments of your choice once you've arrived at your travel destination.

Age

Some women believe they are too old to travel solo—"too old" being anywhere between thirty and ninety years of age. We live in a youth-obsessed culture in which women are told they should start to feel old from age thirty—the age when the biological clock picks up speed and the reality of declining fertility is reluctantly realized. By the age of forty all advertising and media deny our existence, and when they do include "women of a certain age," these dames look fantastic and are so unlike any women in our cohort of friends we question whether they have been genetically modified like the tomatoes and strawberries found in supermarkets. Stop participating in this! Banish expressions such as, "At my age I'm too old to [insert activity here]." Such expressions become self-fulfilling prophecies. If you actually believe sixty is old, you'll adopt that way of thinking and become completely inactive. If you choose to celebrate the many benefits of aging instead—yes, there *are* benefits—you will create an optimistic mind-set. For example, while I hate the changes my body is experiencing during menopause (hot flashes, declining bone density, flabby skin, graying hair, wrinkles and lines), I choose not to dwell on them and focus instead on the benefits of being a woman in her fifties (no periods and therefore fewer hormonal changes and mood swings, heightened energy, more money, increased confidence, more time for myself). Women can travel at any age, as long as they have the right attitude.

Many women have an image of the lone female traveler as a thin, suntanned, twenty-something backpacker, with sandals, numerous tattoos, minimal underwear, and sun-bleached hair; they see no relationship between this Aphrodite and their post-menopausal being. The few mainstream guidebooks that consider solo travel and women contribute to this image by addressing issues such as coping with menstruation on the road and unwanted sexual predation, while at the same time failing to discuss the need for frequent bathroom breaks and therapeutic insoles, hence alienating again the older cohort. If you go at your own pace, schedule rest time, wear sensible footwear, and adjust any itinerary to personal health and fitness needs, nothing should stop you. When I was in Berlin a few years ago, I walked for three hours then had excruciating pain in my foot, later diagnosed as plantar fasciitis. This was devastating—I've enjoyed every city I've visited primarily by walking. Suddenly my few days in Berlin were in jeopardy. That afternoon I limped to the only boat cruise operating and sulked (it was March and not peak tourism time). But in hindsight the event had three effects: first, it forced me to acknowledge my body was aging and that I could not treat it as I had in the past; second, it necessitated an alteration of plans—I took transit more, rented a bike (leading to the fantastic discovery that Berlin has superb cycle routes), and visited numerous coffee shops. I still saw Berlin, but not primarily on foot; finally, it made me realize there are hundreds of places I want and need to visit while physically fit, and that I shouldn't wait until the kids have left home, the mortgage has been addressed, and the orthodontic work paid for. No more procrastination! Age should not prevent travel; plans just need to reflect physical abilities.

Money and Time

Related to family commitments is the barrier of money and time. The issue of money needed to travel depends on your own individual circumstances. The single woman in control of her own finances has only to justify to herself the need to direct money to travel, whereas a woman with a partner and/or family may feel guilty spending some of the collective income on a solo trip. If single, the issue becomes one of priorities: Will you purchase a new car/outfit/sofa/computer, or will you pay for an excursion? If you're single, you can probably find the time. If you are in a relationship, follow the same advice as offered above when discussing family commitments. You may feel guilty (there's that word again!) spending money on a solo holiday, but by illustrating to your family how a brief vacation would not infringe significantly upon the family's finances, you can reduce the guilt. Alternatively, ask your loved ones for an indulgent break—a night or two away in a nice hotel in an adjacent city—as a birthday/Christmas gift; pay the expenditure from an existing savings account, or sell something (such as an inherited family heirloom that you do not use or like) to fund the trip. Think creatively, or just tell those with whom you share financial decisions you will be spending a specific amount on a vacation for yourself within the next six months. Then simply do it.

Small vacations away from our regular routines and

commitments are great ways to de-stress. Women are expected to take on a number of different tasks and as a result have the reputation of being far more organized than the opposite sex. Use this organizational ability—presuming you do have it—to create the time you keep telling yourself is not there.

Personal Safety

In another life I was a criminologist. My PHD and MA degrees are in criminology with a specialization in policing. For ten years I studied extensively, worked, and published in the field of crime for the Royal Canadian Mounted Police and police agencies in two countries and for government and academic bodies. My first book, *Introduction to Policing in Canada*, was published almost twenty years ago and is still used today. I know a thing or two about crime and, what is highly relevant here, the fear of crime. While a few words in this book may be embroidered for effect, this section comes from the heart and is grounded in years of academic study. It is imperative you pay attention to this section, more so than any other. Rant over. Read on.

Tell some people you plan to travel solo and their immediate retort will be to inform you of a friend of a friend of a friend who got stalked/robbed/attacked/all three on a recent trip and returned a shivering wreck and without part of their anatomy. Crime does happen, but the cities I recommend traveling to are statistically a lot safer than the North American town to which the majority of us pay taxes. Despite this, many women fear traveling solo because they fear victimization. Fear and apprehension are perfectly normal emotions and are good in moderation if accompanied by awareness. Your ability to overcome this fear and not let it prevent or curtail your actions is crucial. Many travel writers have addressed the issue of safety for women; inevitably they all argue that the single woman must avoid taking unnecessary risks, adopt a confident stance, and walk purposefully, with head held high, to deter any approaches. The aura this woman exudes is key. Fear should not preclude travel and yet it seems to be the one thing that prevents most women from taking flight (see "Staying Safe").

Much of this articulated fear arises when solo travel is a new undertaking. Overcoming apprehension does not necessitate a huge two-week vacation to a remote South Seas island. For those who have never spent a night away from home alone, keep it simple and plan an easy overnight trip. Start small and travel in incremental steps. Choose a destination easily accessible from home by car, train, or bus. Arrive in time for lunch, book into a hotel, explore for twenty-four hours, and return home the following evening. During that time, you will have been forced to travel alone, arrange accommodations, sleep in an unfamiliar bed, eat by yourself, and explore without company. Something may go wrong, but it's most likely that everything will proceed without any issues and there will not be enough time to get lonely. The biggest surprise will probably be how easy and safe traveling solo is, coupled with regret that this step was not taken earlier. Return and tell your family and friends. Let the travel bug bite and plan your next, longer sojourn.

By carefully selecting the destination, you can overcome any rampant excuses and fears that solo travel is not a safe option. If troubled by language issues, visit a city or country where English is spoken, even if it's with a radically different accent, though with a similar culture. Likewise, if getting lost is a big concern, cities such as New York or London are not the best choices, whereas Savannah or Edinburgh (significantly smaller populations, no metro system, and a reputation for being walkable) are. People with a fear of flying or concern about driving in a strange place should explore train and bus options. Read travel books, do online research, and soon the geographical layout of your chosen destination will become familiar—*before* your arrival—giving you confidence to make the booking. Talk to supportive family members and friends about ambitions. Rent DVDs or download travel guides and shows. Research and planning the proposed trip will help you gain confidence and engender excitement and commitment. Planning and anticipation can be half the fun.

──➤ SUMMARY

The most frequent excuses for not traveling solo include a reluctance to leave family, loneliness, dining alone, age, lack of money or time, and worry about personal safety. All these barriers are real, but by acknowledging and understanding them, they can be addressed.

Now, with all these barriers—and solutions for addressing them—in mind, I will be the first to admit solo travel is stressful. Transatlantic or cross-country travel between time zones leads to jet lag and fatigue. Choosing routes between airports and hotels at godforsaken hours is challenging as you have to analyze whether the taxi driver is trustworthy or if they're the axe murderer your conservative friend back home warned you about. Unexpected delays, especially when traveling during winter, disrupt even the most well-researched plans. Sleeping in unfamiliar beds, walking unaccustomed distances, eating at odd times, and navigating around a new city for hours on end adds to the tension and will leave a mark.

Yes, there will be lows, but in my experience these are generously exceeded by highs. Solo travel is not all wonderful, but for every negative there are numerous positives. Unfortunate events, while distressing at the time, can be easily forgotten—just try to relax and accept unanticipated events and you'll soon bounce back. Think of all the things you've done alone; traveling is not that different. So look forward to tomorrow and cultivate an optimistic outlook. As with all life events, we can fully appreciate them only in retrospect. The confidence you gain from traveling alone will pay off in spades once you return home.

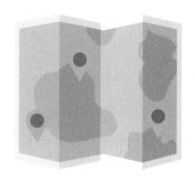

PLANNING YOUR TRIP

Don't tell me how educated you are—tell me how much
you traveled.

—Author unknown

———▸ **HALF THE FUN IS NOT** getting there—it's planning *how* to
get there. Researching a proposed trip, deciding when and
where to go, discussing it with family and friends, making the
booking, and counting the days are just as important as actually
being there. Researchers from the Netherlands found the act of
planning a vacation boosts happiness for a period of eight weeks
prior to the proposed trip, but afterwards happiness levels drop
to "normal" levels. They concluded taking two one-week trips is
preferable to taking one two-week trip because the true benefit
of a holiday is the anticipation. Anticipation has real, positive

effects on the psyche. When I was a little girl, I cried every Christmas Day; the actual event never lived up to my expectations and was less satisfying than the anticipation leading up to it. Other women have conveyed the same story. Excitement is a wonderful, youthful emotion sometimes lost as we get older, but the anticipation of travel can restore it.

If this is your first trip alone, it's probably better to decide not to go halfway around the world for a three-week camel trek, no matter how much of a good deal it seems. This may seem far-fetched, but a few years ago I found accommodations in Australia for $1.25 per night—very tempting—but once I read the small print I realized this was the rate for shared accommodations on a camel ranch with some vague expectation of "pitching in." Start small; build up travel experiences and the confidence to do more. Book a night or two in a city or community you can easily and confidently reach by car, plane, train, and/or bus. Visit the local library or bookstore to read about the various possibilities and determine what's appealing, or go online and read blogs and local tourist information websites and visit convention center sites. Ask your friends where to go, and talk to anyone who's visited the places you're interested in. Talking about your dreams turns them from ideas and intentions to realities. "I really want to go to Rome" becomes "When I go to Rome" and eventually "When I was in Rome." Telling others means they will ask about your travel dates, which will add to the inevitability of the excursion and your commitment to take flight. It's a bit like deciding to lose weight: if you tell everyone you plan to lose ten pounds in the next two months, there is more pressure to do so. There's nothing worse than failing when your intention has been publicly stated.

If this is a first-time-ever solo trip the aims are twofold: to see a new place and be a tourist and, more importantly, to prove to yourself you can do it. The confidence and experience you'll gain from this will establish the belief that this will be the forerunner to many more journeys, hopefully to places farther afield and for longer periods of time. Of course, you can decide on a location because of passions and interests—Boston in the USA if you adore history, Edinburgh in Scotland if you're intrigued by castles, or Budapest in Hungary if you love spas. Whatever motivates you to choose a destination, remember to factor in the costs of activities. It's also important to consider energy levels and fitness. Is walking and exploring eight hours a day feasible, or would it be better to walk, return to the hotel and take a nap, and then explore again?

Speaking of managing your energy: while there's nothing wrong with city-hopping and hitting a number of different locations (e.g., Seattle, Portland, and San Francisco, or Budapest, Prague, and Vienna), constantly changing hotels, packing and unpacking, and moving on to the next place adds to exhaustion. That's why I believe it's preferable to spend at least three nights in the same place. With a bit of time, the hotel room becomes a real home—your books are on the bedside table, the refrigerator's stocked, and you become familiar with the surroundings, both within and adjacent to the hotel. What's more, staying in one location prevents loneliness: you get to know staff and surroundings, and with your clothing out of the suitcase and hung in the closet, a sense of ownership of the location emerges.

Once you've decided on a destination, the next step is to pinpoint when you want to go and for how long. If not confined to certain times of the year, choose not to visit in peak season.

Visiting during Christmas holidays, Thanksgiving, school summer holidays, or when the area is too hot or too cold can easily be avoided if you are free to travel whenever you choose. During certain times of the year, the price of flights and accommodations doubles or triples—for example, avoid Boston during the weekend of the Boston Marathon, or Montreal during the Jazz Festival, unless you specifically want to attend; accommodations will be at a premium, prices will be high, and the city will be loud. Consider visiting certain cities in the winter; it can be challenging, but there will be fewer crowds. All told, choosing what time to visit is an important decision.

Next, decide on your budget. How much do you have to spend on this holiday? Are you comfortable at a two-star motel, or do you require five-star luxury? Transatlantic flights are not cheap, especially during the summer, and Europe tends to be more expensive in every aspect than North America: free refills of coffee are not available, for example, so for those of us accustomed to multiple early-morning cups of caffeine, the cost quickly ratchets up; on the upside, alcohol tends to be cheaper. (For every cloud . . .)

When you've decided on destination (or destinations—there's nothing wrong with looking at alternatives), length of trip, time of year, and budget, go to some well-known websites and spend a few hours researching online. Or, if you are not comfortable using the Internet, visit a travel agency such as Flight Centre and let it do the work; choose a time when the agency is not busy (weekdays, avoiding lunchtime). Travel agents have a wealth of knowledge, as they spend their days researching the best locations in the world, alternative ways to access them, and the ways to enjoy them. Such agents also have a close relationship with providers are therefore sometimes have access to discounts and upgrades. Most agents offer their expertise for free, and using their services is a good option for people who do not have the time to look for holidays, have specific needs (flower arranging in Tuscany, hiking in Mongolia), or just feel more confident using a professional. Remember, looking for holidays is the first step. This is just the research stage; you're just browsing. Treat a travel purchase like a shoe purchase. What sane woman ever bought the first pair of shoes tried? Explore a number of alternatives before making the final decision. No one is watching. Make it fun and educational.

The websites I use are Expedia (www.expedia.com) and Travelocity (www.travelocity.com); they're similar in price, format, and content, and are easy to navigate. I've been using Expedia for about ten years and have never had any issues. These services have really good customer relations as well, so if you do have to call them, they can usually address concerns. I never book immediately—instead I spend a couple of days visiting and revisiting the site, thinking about the alternatives, reading the reviews (although recently the quality and relevance has been called into question) and sleeping on it. Trip Advisor (www.tripadvisor.com) and many other websites provide reviews of hotels. A word of caution, though: avoid promotions that offer discounts for booking accommodations and flights together. Decide on the best flight options, then the accommodations, and see if savings can be made if booked together. You may find a better deal if the flight is booked directly with the airline and the hotel at another website. I book flights first, then car rental/local transportation if needed, then accommodations. A week prior to departure I check and recheck to ensure all bases have been covered. I run through the logistics to confirm such things as arrival time, how to get from the airport to hotel, currency, whether the hotel has been prepaid, whether I have to pay additionally for Wi-Fi, parking, etc.

When making the decision to take flight, be completely honest with yourself about what you want to gain by travel. What are your highest priorities? Do you need a complete break, and do you want to simply to sit on a beach and read? Do you want to cross the continents or remain closer to home? Do you have a desire to see other cultures, have an adventure, or develop a hobby or interest? How important are accommodations? Would you be content in a hostel with a shared bathroom down the hall, or do you need five-star luxury? Do you want to plan everything yourself or use a travel agent? Should a first-time trip take the form of an organized, structured cruise or tour, or do you need to march to the beat of your own drum? In asking all these questions, what I hope to facilitate in offering guidance and advice is a passion to travel solo, whatever your age and ambitions, but at the end of the day the decision is entirely your own.

⟶ GETTING THERE

Unless you plan to drive your own car, there are basically three options for travel: train/bus, car rental, and air.

Train/Bus Travel

Train travel in the USA (or to the USA) can be reviewed by using the Amtrak website at www.amtrak.com, and in Canada at the VIA Rail website at www.viarail.com. Both offer senior discounts, advance booking discounts, and have a number of special offers throughout the year. These companies both offer complete vacation packages as well as travel-only options.

Traveling by train in both Canada and the USA can be very, very slow; furthermore, delays are common, so you need to not want to get to your destination in a hurry. Also, the trains can get busy, but for a few additional dollars, business class can be worth the additional expense. Check the rates—there may not be service to your desired city at specific times of the year. Both countries offer superior service and choice on the Eastern Seaboard and the Maritimes to reflect the density of population, but many destinations, some quite sizable (such as Las Vegas), are not served by rail. Train travel is very relaxing and well priced in the USA, but in Canada VIA Rail is more costly, often more expensive than flying. If traveling by bus, look into local companies in your state or province; if traveling farther afield, contact Greyhound (www.greyhound.com and www.greyhound.ca). While Greyhound is convenient and economical, the trips can be long with numerous stops; again, it is often more economical to fly. Bus journeys in the winter can be affected by the weather. Also, be aware of the time of arrival, as some bus and train stations in North America are not situated in the most desirable areas of town and can be, or appear to be, threatening at night. Factor in late arrival, and plan how you'll get from the train or bus station to your accommodations.

In contrast to train travel in North America, that in Europe is a totally different ball game. With an intricate network of high-speed rail lines criss-crossing the continent, it's easy to travel between European cities. Europe has invested in its ability to convey residents and tourists from one country to another or from one city to the next, and it has a reputation for a smart, efficient service. Train travel in Europe is convenient, fast, and affordable, and provides excellent service to the single woman traveler. I love train travel there because you can see so much: little villages, fields, churches, industry—and you can meet or observe interesting, diverse people. I always choose this option if available. A few years ago, I had to go to the Austrian village of Wöllersdorf (population 4,000, but I suspect they count the cattle in this number), about an hour by train from Vienna, to meet a potential new customer. The Canadian government offers a service to assist Canadian companies to gain export sales, and a helpful bureaucrat in Ottawa named George had provided detailed instructions on train travel from Vienna to Wöllersdorf and beyond. I was the only passenger getting off the train at Wöllersdorf. Standing alone on the long platform, I watched the train disappear and wondered if any North American women with nail polish and high heels had ever been here. There were no taxis. There were no cars. There was, however, a lot of cattle and the noise of clunking cowbells.

Upon arrival at the station, all I needed to do, according to George, was take a taxi to meet my customer. At Wöllersdorf Station I found six houses, all with wooden skis above the doorways as decoration, along with unpaved roads and three meadows full of cattle, with cows that had bells around their necks. I walked to the only building, where I discovered an Austrian rail employee in a red waistcoat and a smart, matching hat with a logo—and he spoke impeccable English. This delightful (though very formal) man told me he could call for a taxi, which would take about forty-five minutes to arrive. He then stated my appointment was only about a twenty-minute walk away and enthusiastically suggested I walk; I suspect he advised this because he was keen to clear his nice neat platform of anyone resembling a customer. Dressed in a dark blue business suit and expensive, uncomfortable shoes, I walked on the deserted dusty roads to discover my potential customer, cursing George and Industry Canada the whole way. After the meeting I walked back, greeted the waistcoated Austrian, and sat in the sunshine in the deserted station, where I admired the flower boxes, listened to the cowbells, and waited over an hour for a train to Vienna. While initially stressful, this unique experience confirmed again my love of solo travel.

If using trains in Europe, access the website of the train companies in the country you are visiting (Germany, England, France, etc.) and search the larger sites that provide information about train travel between European countries, such as www .eurail.com, www.raileurope.com, and www.thetrainline.com. These larger sites can also give information about rail passes. If you order a ticket online, you must collect it from a kiosk at the European train station itself before departure (unless paying an additional delivery fee), which is safe and convenient. Confirmation of the booking will be sent to you by email with a reference number to obtain the ticket at the station. Prices for the same rail journey can vary significantly; book in advance to get the best rates. The rates offered by the larger rail sites are often more expensive than the rates offered by the smaller country-specific sites, even for the exact same journey, so compare prices. Prices can also range considerably between the same locations on different days of the week and at different times of the day, so if you're flexible, bargains can be had, for example, by traveling at 1 PM on a Tuesday rather than 5 PM on a Friday.

If considering a trip to Europe that involves two cities (e.g., Paris and Amsterdam, Budapest and Vienna), it's often more convenient to travel between those two destinations by rail rather than by plane, as the railway station will most likely be within the city, unlike the airport. Be forewarned: many cities have more than one railway station (Brussels, for example has three, Paris six). The biggest disadvantage with European rail travel is that some routes are very crowded, especially on Friday and Sunday afternoons, so avoid these times if possible. Also, traveling with heavy or large pieces of luggage can be an issue. With this in mind, consider traveling business class, and always book a seat if possible. Trains are a great place to meet people and to see the countryside from a relaxed position. Many have cell-phone-free compartments, so the woman speaking loudly to her husband by phone as she gives him instructions on where he can find the only red onion in the kitchen can be avoided. I've also found that train patrons are generally polite and accommodating to lone female tourists who look a little lost, and will often help with luggage and offer advice. The only exception to this, I found, was when traveling on Eurostar between Paris and London (not a cheap rail option); the man I was seated next to in the fully reserved compartment decided to read a pornographic magazine. Odd reading material for public transport! While I initially found this a little unnerving, we both ignored each other and the journey unfolded much the same as any other.

In most European cities, buses offer cheaper options than the train and flights. A myriad of bus companies operate across Europe, many specific to one country (for example, National Express in the UK); others operate service within the country and between European centers. See www.europebuspass.com and www.eurolines.com to research routes, timetables, and costs.

Car Rental

Car reservations should be made as soon as the dates of the vacation have been set. It costs nothing to make a booking and cancel it prior to the reservation date, so if at a later date a better rate becomes available, cancel and rebook. Car rental prices, like hotel fees, increase as the date requiring the service gets closer, but can dip two to three weeks from the required date, depending on demand. Keep in mind as well that fees are always considerably higher during the summer months. When making your reservations, consider using a booking website such as Expedia—there you can compare rates between different companies (e.g., Hertz, Avis, National); there's actually little to no benefit gained by using their individual websites. Keep in mind, too, that it's easier to collect a car *at the airport* rather than taking a shuttle bus to the agency's location, usually adjacent to the airport (sometimes it's necessary to wait thirty minutes for this shuttle bus to show up, especially during the evening, but in larger airports, such as London's Heathrow and those in, Rome, Las Vegas, and Denver, there is no alternative). You can find car rental locations for each airport on Expedia's website. Frequently it is more economical to catch a taxi to the city and rent a car from the city center rather than from the airport, as rental companies charge a premium for rental from an airport. Check whether the car has unlimited mileage and avoid those that do not have this option—the rental can increase significantly if charged per kilometer driven. Collecting a car from one location and returning it to another also incurs an additional charge, which can be quite significant. Many credit card companies offer car insurance with gold cards; if you rent cars on a regular basis, a gold credit card is worthwhile, although in my experience all rental agencies still try to sell you their own insurance.

When renting, always check for bumps, dents, and scratches when you're picking up the vehicle—and perform this check in a well-lit area; you could find yourself in a dark parking lot after twilight, or in an underground car park, so be careful. In North America I have found rental agencies are flexible about little nicks and scratches, but in other jurisdictions (and in the UK and Italy especially) rental agencies are zealous in their review of returned vehicles, checking over every inch. Cars in Europe tend to be smaller than in North America; many are manual drive (a premium is charged for automatic) and driving on busy, winding, unfamiliar, crowded streets after a long flight can be stressful.

When getting the keys, spend time familiarizing yourself with the car in the rental lot before driving away. Place your luggage in the trunk and ensure your purse is close at hand (for road tolls) and that drinking water is accessible. Adjust the seat and check mirrors for alignment and visibility, and find reverse gear. This may sound obvious, but a few years ago I rented a manual car in the UK, drove for two hours, and parked the car in a crowded car park. When it was time to leave I could not find reverse gear, so I had to draw on the expertise of a man in the car park, which of course confirmed his opinion of women drivers.

As I travel a lot, rental agencies often want to offer me an upgrade, usually to a much larger salesman-type executive car. While many would deem this a perk, I do not. Smaller cars are easier to park, more economical on gas, easier to drive, and better for the environment—and as there is only me in the vehicle, I don't need the luxury of more power or space.

If renting a car after a long flight or when arriving tired, have a caffeinated beverage, keep the car cool, take breaks, and do not be distracted by the radio or music until familiar with the vehicle. If arriving at an airport in the evening, consider staying at an airport hotel rather than driving a strange car on unfamiliar roads for long distances in the dark.

For many women and men, driving abroad is taking adventure one step too far, especially if the roads are left-hand drive (UK, Australia, and New Zealand) or small and winding (Europe). And no matter how prepared you are, you must expect the unexpected. I have hundreds of disastrous car rental stories: I left the airport in Boston without any change in my purse, eventually causing a huge traffic jam—during rush hour *and* in the rain—at the automated toll; I drove into the taxi car park at Denver airport and couldn't exit; I put diesel fuel into a non-diesel car in Lisbon; I couldn't find the rear window wiper shut-off button, thus driving for two hours with a noisy blade scraping a dry window (I did what any woman would have done in this instance and turned up the volume on the CD player); I locked my keys in the car and needed the Royal Canadian Mounted Police to rescue me in Golden, British Columbia; I ran over and murdered six ducklings in New Zealand as their mother looked on. I could go on. Again, it's a confidence thing. I find driving in Australia, New Zealand, Canada, and the USA easy, but in Europe it's a lot more stressful. GPS has made navigation easier, but there are still issues. And remember, city center hotels charge significant rates for car parking, adding considerably to the cost of rooms.

Air Travel

I do not complain about air travel as it grants me what I desire most: to rapidly be somewhere else. Even better, as an airline passenger I have no decisions to make—a unique and welcome luxury in the life of a solo traveler. I'm told where to sit and with whom, what and when to eat and drink, when to sleep, and when I can and cannot move. I have no control over delays or arrival times. My life is totally in the hands of others. How often does this occur in our day-to-day lives?

Let me put one misconception to rest: there is no perfect time or day to book a flight. Some travel literature says Tuesday is the best day, but recently others have suggested airlines reduce their fees on Saturday. Booking early and being flexible are the only reliable strategies in the never-ending quest to secure the best fare and seat. Selecting a flight can be a real minefield, and trusting that you've negotiated the best price can be stressful, so after you make your booking *do not check* if the price of the flight has altered. This will just be depressing if you find it's been reduced. The cheapest flight will always include multiple changes and long layovers and cannot be cancelled or changed. Check the cost benefit. For example, during a recent Expedia search I found I could get from my home in Vancouver, Canada, to Las Vegas within three hours on a direct flight for $400 return; alternatively, for $275 I could get there but would have to change aircraft twice, spend nine hours traveling, and leave at 5 AM. The first option would be six hours door to door, the second over twelve with more possibilities for delays and lost luggage. The $125 saving is the price of one (or two) nights of hotel accommodations in Vegas. This is therefore a personal decision based on time and finances. It's not easy. If not confined to specific dates, enter different departure dates to see if there are fluctuations in price—for example, it's often more reasonable to fly on a Saturday as there is no business travel. And look out for seat sales: charter airlines often have discounts on flights about three weeks prior to departure. The aforementioned travel sites (Expedia, Travelocity) search the various airlines for the best deals. If they mix and match airlines (such as American Airways with Air Alaska flights), large baggage will not be tracked to the final destination and will need to be collected at the connecting airport. In addition to giving a price, these websites also give travel times, including connections. Be wary if the connection time is under sixty minutes. It is much better to go with what makes you comfortable—and remember, many North American hub airports (Chicago, Houston, Denver) and European airports (Heathrow, Frankfurt, Amsterdam) are huge; navigating from one side to the other, changing terminals, clearing customs if arriving in the European Union, seeking out a restroom, getting a bottle of water takes time. Add to this the initial task of deplaning with stressed fellow passengers who, in my experience, inevitably travel with and are responsible for an extended family consisting of old, slow, deaf, wheelchair-bound parents and two sets of hyperactive twins under the age of five in addition to multiple pieces of hand luggage. I have found making a connection often takes considerably more than the sixty minutes Expedia has naïvely allocated to the task.

While websites list all commercial airlines, they frequently do not include the charter ones, which are often cheaper. These charter airlines, such as Air Transat (www.airtransat.ca), which flies from a number of large Canadian cities to European cities, or Virgin America (www.virginamerica.com), can save you hundreds of dollars in transatlantic flight costs. In June 2015 I flew from Vancouver to Glasgow on a charter flight for $900.

The Air Canada or British Airways flight would have cost me over $1,600. In Europe there are a large number of these cheaper charter airlines (e.g., www.easyjet.com, www.ryanair .com, www.jet2.com, www.cityjet.com) operating between cities not quoted on Expedia's and Travelocity's websites. These no-frills airlines may appear to offer a good deal but often charge an additional fee for stowed luggage on European flights, fly to smaller airports on the outskirts of the destination offer only a few flights per week, have non-refundable and non-changeable tickets, and cut service in the winter months. All North American carriers now demand payment for checked baggage for domestic flights but have not (yet) incorporated a fee for transatlantic flights.

After booking, print a copy of the receipt and ticket; check and recheck that everything is correct—it's much easier to correct a mistake when it's just occurred than a few days prior to departure. At this time it is also possible to book a seat, but there may be a charge. Alternatively, seats can be booked twenty-four hours before the flight at no cost, and a boarding card can be downloaded to your phone or printed out at home.

As everyone readily acknowledges, airline seats are shrinking as North American hips are growing; unless you can afford business class, air travel is uncomfortable. My one piece of advice about seat selection is this: aircraft fill up from the front, so if there are any spare seats these will be at the back of the plane in the central section. When traveling on a transatlantic flight, I book an aisle seat at the back of the plane, as this is the location most likely to have an adjacent spare seat. On the downside, passengers occupying these seats will be the least likely to have a choice of meals and will be last to exit the aircraft.

Travel agents can, of course, research airlines and give advice. For those who prefer to talk to a real person, this option is always available.

⟶ STAYING THERE

While booking flights can be regarded as a minefield, it's easy when compared to looking for accommodations in a strange new city. There are, however, a few simple rules to follow. Decide on the region of the town or city you want to stay in and look for lodging there. Most cities have distinctive areas near the tourist attractions where hotels are concentrated. While a four-star hotel with pool and gym in Rome may look like a bargain at $160 a night, once you find it requires a forty-minute subway journey into the central part of the city (requiring at least ninety minutes of precious tourist time to commute, along with additional financial cost) it may not seem that attractive. Read guidebooks and check online to determine the best regions in which to book accommodations. Many hotels give location information on their website and specify their distance from major attractions. Some guidebooks such as the Lonely Planet series provide comparisons between different areas in cities, but tend to do so only for larger cities such as London and New York.

Use the online search engine filters. A search for "Paris and vicinity hotels" on Expedia will produce almost 1,900 alternatives, but searching by the region "Latin Quarter" with the filter "three star or more" will narrow the results to a more manageable 35 alternatives.

Read the online reviews. Recently a number of newspaper articles and bloggers have questioned the reliability of these reviews. I think they should all be taken with a pinch of salt. They can be useful, for example, when they state, "close to square, so noisy at night" or "get to breakfast early as they run out." If more than four reviewers state the same issue, such as "air conditioning not working," I tend to believe them.

Be aware of cultural differences. Many North American reviews complain about the size of European bathrooms and beds, but European travelers are familiar with this and do not question it; all rooms are small in Europe, and old, noisy plumbing is not uncommon. If these things matter to you, upgrade. (I recently sought a hotel in London and could not find a review for a three-star establishment that rated greater than 3.2 out of 5, so I decided to invest in an additional $50 per night to upgrade to a four-star with a 4.5 rating.) European bed and breakfasts often do not have en suite bathrooms but offer shared bathrooms, which may seem quaint for some, but for others can be a pain. Check the small print.

Check if where you're staying has food/room service if the plan is to not eat out. Is there tea and/or coffee available in the room? Is there a fridge and/or a microwave?

After researching and deciding on the hotel on a travel website (such as Travelocity), visit the hotel's site and see if you can get a better deal. This site will also give more information about the hotel and may have more room options and useful advice upon accessing the hotel from the airport/railway station.

While there are a large number of international hotel chains (e.g., Hilton, Ramada, Sheraton), which provide a uniform standard, my preference has always been Best Western (www.bestwestern.com); each one is independently owned but offers a taste of the culture of the city/country visited. I have stayed in Best Western hotels in about ten different countries and have yet to be disappointed. If booking through a search engine and through the hotel online booking system, there is usually an area for special requests before the booking is completed. Therefore, if you expect to arrive at the hotel very late, this can be detailed. If the choice is between two double beds or one king-sized, you can state this preference. I tend to request a quiet room away from the elevators and not above the bar, and always end my request with a "thank you for your attention" comment in an attempt to get on the good side of the individual making this decision.

Payment can be taken in advance or upon arrival, with the option of payment in local currency or US/Canadian dollars. If paying in advance, keep a copy of the receipt in case the hotel has no record of payment. This document also ensures the expected services are included (free Internet, breakfast, late checkout, etc.). Make sure to keep the confirmation of the booking, even if you haven't paid in advance.

One of the better services for single women is the provision of hotel-recommended taxis or shuttle services to and from airports. Once you've booked the hotel, contact their customer service representatives directly and give them your arrival time and departure time to arrange this service and to confirm the price. Hotels offering a complimentary shuttle service from the airport may provide significant savings, because taxis will not be needed, but beware: I once booked a hotel with a "free shuttle" only to be told upon arrival this shuttle needed to be booked two weeks in advance—another illustration of unanticipated expense.

Decide how you plan to move around the city. If public transport is on the agenda, a hotel outside the center may be the preferred option; if you intend to walk, book accommodations near attractions. Locate public transit if your hotel is not in the center of town.

If exercise is important, select a hotel with a fitness center and/or pool/hot tub. Be aware that sometimes the facilities in cheaper hotels are not all that great, with pools the size of postage stamps and broken, old exercise equipment. If these services are good, they provide a safe opportunity to socialize with fellow travelers.

When you book in and see the room, check it out before unpacking. If something is not right, return to reception and politely ask for the issue to be resolved or to change rooms. The decor and bathroom furnishings are usually great, but I often have issues with the air conditioning, water pressure, and electricity. I once complained about the heat in my expensive German hotel: the windows could not be opened and the temperature was not controlled in the room itself. The hotel's response was to give me a basket of fruit—totally useless! The same scenario happened in Chicago where my room was above the kitchen; the carpet was literally hot to walk on. On this occasion I was upgraded to a suite. Hotels generally accommodate guest wishes as long as they have the space to do so and the request is reasonable and politely made.

Wi-Fi is now becoming a standard free service in most hotels, but a few do still charge. If this is the case, consider accessing free Wi-Fi service in adjacent coffee bars or at public transportation hubs, community centers, and shops.

In this digital age, it's easy to spend hours looking through hotel reviews, websites, blogs, etc. The amount of information available is stunning, and the Internet-savvy gal can easily get lost and distracted as one search leads to another and another and another. Choosing a place to stay in a new city will in part be a fate thing. Make the decision, place the booking, and do not look back—just get excited.

⟶ BEING THERE

All the cities listed in this book have spawned a wealth of published travel literature. Every major travel book publisher (Fodor's, Moon, Lonely Planet, Rick Steves, etc.) has its own website offering extremely useful pieces of information (see "Further Resources"). Cities' tourism departments also have websites assisting the prospective visitor. If anything, there is too much—not too little—information. Many of these guidebooks provide similar details. In considering how many guidebooks to carry or download to an e-reader, my advice is to review a few from the local library or bookstore or online; whatever one you feel comfortable with is the one to purchase/take/download. I tend to like ones that are not too large; I do not need a list of twenty-five hotels and restaurants, but I *do* want to know what the major attractions are, the days they are closed, and whether reservations are required. I also like guidebooks to have good, colored maps. Tourism leaflets and maps are usually available in the airport arrivals hall or the hotel reception area. Ask the hotel receptionist to mark the location of the hotel on a map, and remember to take a hotel card or leaflet; if you do get lost, you can show it to a taxi driver to ensure a safe return. Sometimes I get a couple of maps and circle the places I want to visit. It may also be useful to note the nearest subway stop. Determine where the tourist information center is located, as this should be your first port of call.

Certain European cities have become such hot spots for main attractions (e.g., Eiffel Tower in Paris, Tower of London, Anne Frank House in Amsterdam) that appointments need to be made well in advance. A visit to the tourist information center ensures reliable information about visiting and often facilitates bookings. If you know the dates of a proposed visit, book in advance online from home.

Many guidebooks provide lists of the top ten attractions, suggested walking tours, and agendas for vacations lasting from two days to two weeks. Use these as a guide to plan your own itinerary. While it is useful to have a core list of must-sees, inevitably it is the unanticipated activities, wanderings, and discovery of buildings, small museums, neighborhoods, and coffee shops not mentioned in the literature that you will find the most rewarding. Before leaving home, research and consider purchasing a "city pass" if your destination city has one; such passes provide discounts on admission to museums and attractions. Calculate if such a pass would be advantageous. Alternatively, when you arrive, purchase one at the tourist office after speaking to the staff there and learning from their experience. Transit passes are also worth considering and are sometimes included with tourist cards, which often give access to museums, galleries, events, etc. at a reduced rate. I always find transit passes more convenient than looking for the correct change and trying to calculate the fare in a foreign land. Standing in front of a machine in a busy transit hub while trying to work out where to place the cash/ credit card and deciding which button to press blatantly advertises you as a tourist. Avoid this as much as possible.

In a new city, my days start with a good breakfast, over which I divide the city up into areas to visit, depending on how many days I have to explore. For example, Prague can be easily split into the "castle" and "old town" areas with a day being dedicated to both; Edinburgh can easily be divided into three distinct areas. Many cities have concentrations of museums (London) or trendy warehouse districts (Portland) or parks (Vancouver, New York), which are must-sees. Most destinations demand a lot of walking, so you should consider bus tours or boat tours in the afternoon when energy levels decline, or any time it's raining. Tours are also desirable upon arrival when you're suffering from jet lag, and are a great way to get a rudimentary understanding of the city. Walking tours tend to be less busy than vehicle tours and make it easy to meet others. Many walking tours in European cities include participants from a vast array of countries, which adds to the attraction. Evening river cruises are a way to meet others over dinner in a non-threatening, welcoming atmosphere. Museums are best seen in the morning when energy levels are higher and crowds lower. Remember, most museums have a day when they close, and also times for free entry.

While I enjoy shopping, I regard it as an activity I can do anywhere, so when traveling it's not on my must-do list. But I do enjoy it at the end of the day when strolling back to my hotel. If I start the day at 9 AM and spend the day walking, I am usually thinking about putting on my pajamas and opening that bottle of wine in my hotel bedroom by around 6 or 7 PM, which is when I find myself drifting into stores to casually shop as the light fades. (I've been known to "casually shop" until 10 PM on Oxford Street in London, on Madison Avenue in Chicago, and in Paris until thrown out of Galleries Lafayette. I am happy to report there were others suffering the same fate.)

Outdoor markets are a lovely way for you to experience local culture and color. If the destination is known for markets and shopping is on your agenda, carry cash, as vendors often do not accept credit or debit cards. Department stores in other cultures offer an interesting contrast to those we have in North America. And prices can be quite different. For example, a shirt at Zara in England can be far more expensive than the exact same garment purchased at Zara in Athens, or Zara in Vancouver. Also, other locations may have more choice in certain attire, reflecting the weather of the location. I purchase sundresses and bathing suits in Las Vegas as I am there every year, and the choice in this hot climate is huge in comparison to the choice at home in colder Vancouver. Other cooler climates have superior choices of boots and winter shoes. If (unintentionally, of course!) your purchases overrun luggage capacity, consider shipping them home by a courier service or purchase a duffel bag and pay for excess luggage—you can justify the expenditure on the uniqueness of the merchandise and/or the bargain gained. Remember, shoe and clothes sizes are different in Europe. Because most clothing is made for the international market, to be sure of sizing check the label in the garment itself, or use a size-conversion website (www .onlineconversion.com or www.asknumbers.com). Some department stores in tourist destinations post size conversion tables.

Although planning any excursion is important, overplanning and rigid agendas limit flexibility and spontaneity, which frequently produce the most entertaining experiences. While it's important to make the most of your time away, seeing world-famous sights, it is often the unanticipated—a museum with a most amazing coffee shop, street performers who keep you entertained for an unscheduled forty-five minute stop, getting lost, torrential rain forcing you to take a bus tour instead of your planned walk in the park—that brings the most joy. Being by yourself means there is only one person to please—you. If at 2 PM you're ravenously hungry and the café overlooking the park is ideal for a two-hour reading break in the sunshine, do it. Enjoy yourself. Do what you want because *you* want to, not because Rick Steves says you should. It's okay to go to Paris for the first time and *not* ascend the Eiffel Tower; there's no shame in staying in Amsterdam without visiting Anne Frank's house; it's perfectly fine to go to London without riding the London Eye. I hate lining up, so I've not visited a multitude of tourist attractions in the cities to which I've traveled; I didn't want to waste time in line. If you're concerned about missing out on the standard tourist sites, remind yourself that you can always return and use your time more productively on the next visit.

While away, it's important to take the rough with the smooth and be flexible. If there's a train strike in France, a snowstorm in Chicago, or even a terrorist alert—all of which require time-consuming waits—be philosophical. I tell myself, *This time tomorrow it will all be over.* I once flew from Europe to Toronto but was rerouted through New York. Five strangers had an additional five-hour wait in New York, where we hunkered down in a bar and shared stories. The time passed in a heartbeat. I missed a day in Toronto but gained new friends.

Traveling by yourself means you answer to no one. No one knows what you're doing. You can choose one day to eat three large gelatos, drink only red wine, and consume no healthy vegetables—it's entirely your decision. In Vienna during the World Cup a few years ago, I found the most amazing outside café that played the televised soccer games on large plasma screens and served huge ice cream sundaes in what looked like glass goldfish bowls. For four consecutive afternoons I went to this café and ordered a different sundae (travel research, right?) and sat watching soccer. After the second day, the waiter saved me a seat and the gelatos increased in size, as did his tip. Perhaps I could have seen more of Vienna, tried different cafés, taken in a few more museums and chateaux, or explored more galleries, but *I did what I wanted to do* and will never forget this time.

→LEAVING THERE

Hopefully returning home will be a positive experience and provide incentive for planning further travel. I am usually invigorated after being away, excited about being reunited with my family, and keen to organize the next trip. I have more energy and am charged with undertaking the tasks home life throws at me. Many, many years ago, I remember returning from a holiday and crying for the better part of two days, because I hated the life I was returning to. At that time my excursion and the emotions upon return provided the catalyst for life-changing action and I left England and moved to Canada. Solo travel should make you a happier individual, but if it does not, and if you have not enjoyed it and found it overwhelmingly stressful, that is fine too. You tried. It can be crossed off your bucket list. It will not be in the "if-only" category anymore.

Travel, especially to foreign cultures, frequently leads to a greater appreciation of home. Often the sheer volume of people in the new cities visited, while exciting for a few days, leads to an appreciation of the quieter, familiar home environment. Expensive coffees, paying to pee, and the constant challenges of navigation in a strange place result in a greater love for familiarity and the area called home. Although I adore the unbridled energy of London, after a week in that city's pollution (the cotton swab I used to cleanse my face each night was thick with black dirt!) I welcome returning to British Columbia's clean air. And while I find driving on narrow French country lanes stimulating, it's also unbelievably stressful, so I appreciate returning home where I can drive in an environment I know well.

If you had a truly excellent time, a slight post-trip cloud is bound to descend, especially when you are quickly catapulted back into the normality of life; bills, emails, cleaning, work, laundry, kids, etc. demand quick adjustment to the real world. Sharing with friends and family stories of your time away can help facilitate the transition back from vacation mode (but remember not to bore them with the two hundred or more photographs you took of the trip, unless they request to see them). Similarly, sorting through photographs of your trip and framing and displaying favorites will remind you of your adventure. But the ultimate tonic is in thinking about and planning the next trip, even if it will be months away—good medicine to cure any post-holiday blues.

─⟶ SUMMARY

Methodical, step-by-step planning and organization are key in making sure you get the most out of an excursion. Therefore, before you choose a destination, make decisions about budget, length of the sojourn, and season. After establishing these fundamentals, research your chosen destination; next, map out the logistics of your arrival, departure, and accommodations, and then check and recheck them. With these tasks completed there are fewer opportunities for things to go wrong. After taking these steps , you must deal with a number of other additional practicalities as the time winds down to the day of departure.

After Deciding to Take Flight

- Ensure your passport is up to date and will not expire.
- Obtain any required visas.
- Make sure any required vaccinations and inoculations are up to date.
- Obtain insurance.
- Book pets into kennels or arrange for friends to care for them. (Kennels often book up early.)
- Start to learn a few words of the language spoken at the destination.
- Prepare your body for the trip; make appointments for any overdue dental and health checkups.

A Month Before You Take Flight

- Consider whether it is desirable to book appointment times at the most popular tourist attractions.
- Obtain currency.
- Notify your credit card provider of the intended travel destination and the dates you will be there.
- Ensure you have the required clothing, and if you need new footwear, buy it in advance so you have time to make sure it's comfortable.
- Review the itinerary to check all modes of transportation and that you have accommodations.
- Make appointments to see dentists, doctors, physiotherapists, and/or hairdressers, if needed.

A Week Before You Take Flight

- Cancel newspaper and mail delivery.
- Check the baggage allowance for the airline.
- Check the weather at the destination.
- Check whether food is provided on the flight.
- Prepare your home and inform neighbors of your absence.
- Book taxis to the airport/train/bus station if needed.
- Start to pack clothes and medical supplies.

The Night Before You Take Flight

- Clean your fridge and remove garbage from your home.
- Lower the thermostat and unplug appliances.
- Check the airline website to ensure the plane is on time.
- Print out your boarding pass.
- Label all luggage securely.
- Check the weather at the destination.
- Get a good night's sleep.

WHAT TO BRING

He who would travel happily must travel light.
　　　　　　　　　　　　　—Antoine de Saint-Exupéry

⟶ **AS EVERY WOMAN KNOWS,** the moment an invite is received—
be it for a friend's wedding, a Christmas party, or a request to
volunteer at the kids' school fair—the biggest decision is what
to wear. A solo trip anywhere raises the same initial questions
but without the same tension. The destination will be filled
with total strangers who do not know you and whom you will
probably never see again. No one cares what you look like.
The stress of what to wear is greatly diminished, if not entirely
eliminated; bad hair days are tolerated, and the lack of lipstick
becomes acceptable, another distinct advantage of solo travel.

When traveling, the key is to have functional clothing and not too much of it. I would love to state that everyone always packs more than they need, but this is not true. As we all know, the opposite sex, and teenage boys especially, do not over-pack. My first piece of advice is to adopt the mindset of a teenage boy when you are thinking about what to pack; if you can do this, packing for any excursion should be a breeze.

──→ LUGGAGE

As I travel a lot, I have a wide variety of good-quality luggage in varying sizes and colors (not black). My favorite mid-size red suitcase has been with me over fifteen years and is still going strong. Invest (or borrow) reliable lightweight luggage that will not fall apart, with sturdy zips, retractable handles, and big wheels. Many roads and sidewalks in older European cities are cobblestone, so the suitcase needs to be tough to withstand being pulled over this bumpy terrain. Use the smallest suitcase possible, unless you anticipate purchasing a lot while away. Whenever I travel to Europe I want to return with cheeses, so I leave enough room to bring these back to North America, and sometimes upgrade my flight for increased weight allowance. Practice carrying luggage up and down stairs to ensure you can do it. Avoid dollar store luggage labels, as these tend to fall off and will not last a flight; invest in something sturdy. Although quality luggage tags will be far more expensive, they will not need replacing for every journey taken and are of course invaluable should your luggage be lost. Remove all previous airline tags so baggage handlers will not get confused. Many travelers attach bright ribbons or tape to their (usually black) luggage so it is easily recognizable. I think this activity is pointless and shouts "novice traveler" to scam artists and thieves. Avoid having to do this by not purchasing black suitcases to begin with, and by reading the luggage label when pulling your luggage from the conveyer belt. And speaking of thieves: avoid taking expensive jewelry or anything that may look expensive. If concerned about loss, take photographs on your phone so a record is available should the luggage choose to vacation without you.

For hand luggage, I pack my purse in a larger, soft-sided duffel bag with comfy straps and handles. This bag is large enough to accommodate a jacket, sweater, books, neck pillow, food (energy bars, fruit) bottle of water, headphones, and any other items needed on a flight. If you need a coat or heavy boots, wear them or carry them on the flight; don't try to pack them. My purse has essentials such as reading glasses, tissues, medication, tickets, money, passport, and wallet.

→ COSMETICS, TOILETRIES, PHONES, AND ADDITIONAL ITEMS

A strong, waterproof toiletry bag should be large and purchased for function rather than fashion to accommodate a full range of travel-size bottles. Most large drugstores now have areas devoted to travel-size tubes of toothpaste, shampoo, conditioner, Band-Aids, first aid items, etc. These small sizes are also readily available at larger airports. Alternatively, plastic travel-size bottles can be purchased and filled with your favorite products. Ensure the tops are well secured—nothing is worse than discovering your moisturizer is all over the contents of your cosmetics bag. In my toiletry bag I also stash a bottle opener, corkscrew, plastic fork, and spoon for use while snacking in my bedroom.

When I travel to warm destinations, this bag sometimes weighs more than the rest of my luggage and takes up more room. Using North American cell phones in Europe can be expensive, although you can purchase a plan to reduce this expenditure. Check with your provider on the cost of using your own plan abroad. Sometimes it's cheaper to purchase a "pay as you go" phone when staying in your destination country. Wi-Fi tends to be widely available; if you are unlucky enough to stay in a hotel that charges for this service, consider leaving the establishment to access free Wi-Fi, which is widely available in coffee shops, transportation hubs, public leisure centers, and many stores. If you own a very expensive iPhone, consider taking a cheaper phone on the trip. Take only what you can afford to lose.

Sometimes I travel with small gifts from Canada: logo pens, key chains, playing cards, or maple leaf baseball caps for individuals I know I will meet but don't know yet. These people will aid and assist my travel experience: the helpful taxi driver; the receptionist who upgrades my room or fixes the noisy air conditioner; the children of the hotel proprietor who helps me connect with Wi-Fi. These items do not weigh much and never return with me as I inevitably encounter people who make my excursion easier. I give these small tokens of appreciation as thanks for the comfort offered by strangers.

→ CLOTHING

Obviously what you need on holiday will depend on the destination, climate, and length of time away. Often it is difficult, when living in a cold, wet climate, to envisage anywhere else as warm. When traveling to hotter climates, I frequently make the mistake of packing sweaters with the belief that, for example, Athens cannot possibly be eighty degrees in October, and that Google Weather provides wrong information. Three-, seven-, and fourteen-day weather forecasts are available for even the smallest places; use and trust them. (Before you leave, visit www.weather.com or Google the city's name and "weather" to obtain reliable forecasts.)

The most important article of clothing for any excursion is a good pair of walking shoes with non-slip soles. Wear these shoes in before departure to ensure they are comfortable. Running shoes are fine and, in many places, quite the trendy fashion item—for example, in New York, women of every age wear them with dresses, jeans, and skirts. In colder, wetter climates, you'll require sturdier boots. Pack at least two pairs of shoes in case one gets wet, and travel in the heavier ones. For warmer climates I take sandals and runners, which are always useful if I decide to access the gym at the hotel. The second must-have item is an all-purpose, lightweight rain jacket, preferably with numerous zipped pockets and a hood. This will not be a fashion item but should be totally functional, easily packed and carried, and will no doubt last for years.

Traveling alone means you are responsible for carrying luggage. It is easy to overpack, so try to be ruthless. If it's necessary to sit on a case to close it, it's too full. In my experience, clothes expand when traveling, so throw something out. At home I change my shirt daily; when traveling, I wear shirts for two days, but I am the only person that knows and no one else really cares—except maybe the individual at the hotel reception, who after a brief visit I will never see again. This individual will not tell my mother or gossip to my friends. Something I love about returning home from a two-week trip is getting reacquainted with my wardrobe after the time I've spent with the limited contents of a small suitcase.

I begin packing about four days before departure. I started to do this when my children were quite young so they would associate my big red suitcase with Mum's imminent departure, but now it's a habit. Placing articles of clothing into a case ensures they are clean and do not need attention. I also separate the clothes I'll be wearing for the journey so choosing them is not a last-minute decision. I place a limited amount of underwear and socks in a plastic bag and pack additional plastic bags for dirty or damp clothes. Sometimes while away I wash underwear in the bad hotel-provided shampoo and dry it overnight; at other times I buy additional underwear (a real must for any trip to Europe as the store Marks and Spencer has *the* best underwear in the world), and sometimes I pack old underwear and throw it away after use. This last option needs to be discounted if there is even the remotest possibility you could meet the man or woman of your dreams on this trip and that this person has a burning desire to undress you. As this event in my travel life is about as likely as Lancôme calling me to replace Julia Roberts in the latest perfume promotion, I frequently take old grey knickers.

If away for more than a week, I wash clothes with either hotel shampoo or washing powder brought from home. The biggest packing challenge a traveler faces is when a trip involves two distinct activities—for example, a friend's wedding (requiring an entire smart outfit, purse, shoes, gift) and being a tourist (sensible shoes and casual comfortable clothes), or a two-day hike (boots and a backpack) followed by museums and galleries (lightweight clothing). You'd think traveling to hot destinations is always easier with less clothing required, but a few years ago I went to Barcelona for four rainy, cold days in July. After two days I found a second-hand store where I bought an umbrella, sweater, and rain jacket, all of which were totally ugly but functional and were left in Spain upon my return home. Remember, it's always possible to purchase clothes and supplies when away. Thrift stores are everywhere, although they can be difficult to locate when needed, a bit like restrooms.

Layers are important if visiting a city with dramatic changes in day and night temperatures (e.g., San Francisco, Santa Fe). Pack a bathing suit; even if the hotel does not have a pool there may be a hot tub. A comfortable sleeping T-shirt for wandering around the hotel bedroom is also on my required list. Once, in Paris, I was given a freezing cold bedroom in a three-star hotel (the hotel proprietor had obviously slept with someone at the Paris Tourism Office to get this rating) and had to sleep in pajamas, sweatshirt, and two pairs of socks. Be prepared to wear layers.

Re-usable shopping bags fold up and weigh nothing and are also useful when traveling if you need a larger bag than your purse for day-to-day activities and shopping. A number of stores specialize in clothes for traveling (www.tilley.com, www .travelsmith.com, www.columbia.com), but I tend to go with what I already have and feel comfortable in. Dark colors and jeans are a staple. I read Hillary Clinton travels with only a few items of clothing but with a number of scarves to jazz up her wardrobe, so think about adopting the "Hillary" method. Scarves are also useful on a flight or train journey when the air conditioning is on high.

Being an optimist, I never believe my luggage will be lost or delayed, so I don't pack underwear or a change of clothes in hand luggage. If my luggage does suffer this fate, there is nothing I can do about it. The airline will compensate, albeit at a later date. My priority is to enjoy the time away. When younger, I traveled with a finite amount of cash and no Visa card. Now I have credit cards, so if bad things happen, I can address them and will have good material for a "dining out" story upon return.

Every travel book contains an ideal packing list. The school my kids attend provides lists for every excursion they take. But what one needs when traveling is a personal choice. For example, I need instant Starbucks coffee in my hotel bedroom and, accordingly, insist on traveling with little sachets of it. A little bottle of red wine upon arrival in a European hotel after a transatlantic flight helps me sleep and get over the jet lag, so I ensure one is in my suitcase. Still, I've provided a sample packing list (see "Further Resources") with the understanding that every woman's preferences and needs will vary.

STAYING SAFE

Travel is fatal to prejudice, bigotry, and narrow-mindedness.

—Mark Twain

⟶ **AS I HAVE GROWN OLDER**, traveling as a single woman has become a lot easier. There are fewer issues for the fifty-something-year-old than for the twenty-year-old, and not only because the former's level of affluence and number of life experiences are generally greater than the latter's. Young men (statistically the group most likely to commit and be a victim of crime) are less likely to pester, grope, whistle, follow, steal from, or engage in conversation the woman that looks and acts like their mother. Walk confidently by a group of five youths in their early twenties at 6 PM on a crowded tourist street in

Barcelona when you are a twenty-something woman and expect jibes, whistles, cat calls, and unwanted attention. Do the same activity at the age of fifty and experience no reaction; the boys will not even look up. When you are younger and prettier, things happen because you are young and pretty—some good, some bad. When older and wiser, less happens—unless you make it or encourage it to happen.

Being older means being invisible to the opposite sex when traveling and has advantages. Having said that, I recently had an encounter with five European men—all with beautiful broken English accents, and between the ages of fifty-five and sixty-five—on a ferry ride in Scotland. These men were exploring the Scottish Highlands on expensive BMW motorbikes. They invaded my space on the ferry, apologized for doing so, and then proceeded to flirt with me—a fantastic boost to the ego as I unapologetically flirted back. The jovial interaction with my leather-clad entourage involved them making fun of each other, showing me photographs of their families, and offering espresso. If this had happened to a younger woman, this encounter would have had a sexual component. As a mature woman, I find these and the few similar encounters I have had when traveling alone are never sexual (perhaps I have just never been this lucky). It's as if there is a shared sense of "been there, done that" and an understanding and respect of boundaries. Even if I looked like Helen Mirren or had the body of Sophia Loren I would expect the same.

This does not mean traveling alone as a mature female is a breeze. You do need to take precautions, and being observant and vigilant is advisable. Often the most vulnerable time is upon arrival in a new city, especially after a long-haul flight when tired from jet lag and less attentive to details. This is when it's most necessary to check and recheck actions and belongings. It is also the time when those bent on stealing a purse will look for an easy, distracted target. This is the time to invest in a taxi rather than walking ten blocks. Day one in a new, unfamiliar city is stressful because so much is unknown. A few years ago I arrived in Rome for the first time at night. The next morning I left the hotel, and within ten minutes was lost on a quiet, narrow, shadowed street. Looking at a map would identify me as a tourist. I spotted a smartly dressed woman about my age walking with purpose as if heading for work. Like Alice chasing the Mad Hatter down a rabbit hole I caught up with her and started to follow, zigzagging between cars, breaking into a run to catch lights, never more than twenty meters behind my Italian sister. Being in her safe shadow gave me purpose and acquainted me with my new environment, although I did feel creepy following a stranger and not knowing where I was going. She eventually led me to a busy thorough-fare where I had the confidence to check my map and where there were other tourists. Walking behind her for those ten minutes acquainted me with walking in Rome; if she could do it, so could I.

Avoid looking like a tourist. Although some travelers like fanny packs, they scream "stranger" to anyone who cares to notice; recently I read they were deemed one of the least useful travel accessories. Reusable shopping bags with North American logos convey the same message, as do T-shirts advertising US venues and cities. Likewise, examining large maps and looking up at street signs indicate "stranger" in the same way. It is far better to use smaller maps in guidebooks or on a phone, which are way more discreet.

A number of situations promote fear in a traveler. At home, we're usually surrounded by people who are like us—with a similar culture, socioeconomic class, and life experience. When away from home we mix with strangers. This unfamiliar, unknown cohort causes apprehension. Just as we're given the opportunity to address excuses about why we should not travel, so these fears can also be understood, dealt with, and overcome.

→ STREET AWARENESS

You can reduce your chances of being the victim of street crime by choosing to walk in busy urban areas, avoiding back alleys and quiet side streets, and exploring a new city in daylight rather than at night. Being with the local population helps, as does being among women and children. Read the guidebooks and make enquiries at the hotel about any areas you should avoid. Many of these places (parks, gardens, bus and railway stations) are perfectly safe during the day, but more risky at dusk or late in the evening. Be watchful of scam artists on the streets. About five years ago I was on the banks of the Seine in Paris and a young girl walking in front of me bent down and picked something off the ground. As I approached she showed me a lovely gold ring; she put it on her finger but it was too large, so she gave it to me and said I should try it. I did, but after showing me the stamp on the ring, she suggested I give her money for the ring and keep it. I politely rejected her and moved on, not thinking too much about this chance event. Two years later I again found myself in Paris sitting in the famous Tuilleries Gardens. There I watched the exact same scenario unfold for another unsuspecting traveler. Scams such as these are particularly common in popular tourist spots and are not restricted to one country or city. Another common scam is "police officers" asking to check wallets for counterfeit money; a stranger accidentally spilling something near or on you is an age-old ruse to provide distraction while that person, or an accomplice, takes a wallet or purse; another one is smearing toothpaste on your jacket unnoticed, then pointing out this fictional bird's dropping while offering to wipe it away, distracting you as the accomplice focuses on your possessions. Many local police authorities post signs warning of thieves operating in the area when the problem is particularly acute. A common reaction by the tourist upon seeing these signs is to check valuables, which of course shows any observant would-be thief where the loot is stashed.

Scam artists come in every age, gender, and ethnic origin. Just because the woman with the baby looks sweet does not mean she actually is. Likewise, the smart-suited man on the train who flirts with you and speaks impeccable English may seem delightful, but really is just wooing you to get closer to your purse. In Canada, if someone starts to engage me in conversation I make eye contact, enthusiastically carry on the dialogue, and have no preconceived notions of why they are talking to me. If a stranger talks to me when I'm traveling, I politely move away quickly, avoid eye contact, hold onto my purse tightly, say "No, thank you," and leave—even if I'm lost and in need of help. I adopt the same drill I repeatedly told my children: "Do not speak to strangers, no matter how nice." When traveling, I often hate myself for adopting a persona I would never carry at home, but I know it's the wisest choice for self-preservation.

Again, the key here is to, if possible, choose to sit with other women or families. If taking long train rides in Europe or North America, the number of rail employees will ensure safe transportation, and some US rail operators employ security staff in addition to ticket collectors. If taking a bus, choose to sit near the front to be closer to the bus driver. At train or bus stations, avoid badly lit areas (sometimes the restrooms can be a little threatening too). Be particularly vigilant when getting off trains and buses (and leaving airports), as this is when opportunistic predators are more likely to strike. Carry purses and bags across your body, and be advised that backpacks can easily be unzipped on crowded subways, trains, or buses without the owner realizing.

Sometimes the difference in price between a first- and second-class ticket is not considerable, so always check out the first-class option. If you need to take a taxi, ensure it has an operating meter, or negotiate a price with the driver of the vehicle (and not his helpful friend) and write it down before you get into a cab. Travel guides such as the Fodor's series offer advice on how safe taxi travel is in the city under review. If taxi travel is not recommended, ask the hotel to arrange your transportation. It's always preferable to let the hotel staff arrange a taxi, and they will also be able to inform you of the amount you can expect to pay. I tend to believe every tourist gets "taken for a ride" by cabs in Europe. I know I have been, especially upon arrival. Doing research before traveling can prevent this, but at the end of the day it may just be a necessary evil. Finally, avoid getting into nearly deserted subway cars (usually at the ends of the trains); choose the busier ones.

I have never had anyone break into my hotel bedroom, nor has anything gone missing when I have stayed away from home. The arrival of online reviews means many establishments are keen to offer guests a safe, secure sleep. Some hotels do have women-only floors and now market themselves as sensitive to the needs of women (e.g., by providing larger magnifying mirrors in the bathrooms, more lighting, extra hangers in closets, women-only floors), but these tend to be higher-end business traveler's hotels. Any single woman should adopt a few simple procedures when staying at a hotel: always lock the bedroom door; use the do not disturb sign; leave the TV and light on when out so it appears someone is in the room. As many room keys now control electricity, ask for two room keys when checking in so electricity is available when the room is unoccupied. You should never open the door without checking who is knocking, and if you have not ordered room service and are not expecting a visitor, be especially cautious when answering the door. If returning after dark, leave the light on and curtains drawn, and always return to a room with the key in your hand ready to open the door. Do not use the stairs or fire escape, as these are often badly lit and isolated. Avoid rooms that open onto public patios or pools or are on the ground floor. I often decide not to have my room cleaned daily, as I do not feel the need for floors to be washed, towels changed, and bed made, and I hope the person tasked with cleaning my room will be able to go home slightly earlier. As the environmental lobby group becomes more active, many hotels now advertise that sheets and towels are not changed unless guests specifically request this service. Some establishments have started to offer guests incentives for not having their rooms cleaned every day. Finally, if there is not a safe in the room (and there generally is) I lock valuables, few as they are, in my suitcase.

When traveling, trust your instincts. A woman's sixth sense, or gut feeling, or intuition is valuable. We all have it and should use it. If a situation feels wrong, leave. If you do not want to talk to the stranger who wishes to engage in conversation, politely make excuses and walk away. If someone wants to give you something or take you somewhere or believes they have met you before (a popular scam: "I saw you at the hotel this morning") and you do not trust the person, move on. If they think you're rude, it doesn't matter. Remove yourself from the situation. Do not engage in discussion. Tell yourself you have been on the earth x number of years, have survived so far, and can continue to do so now. Adopt a positive, confident demeanor, walk purposefully, sing with your shoulders back, keep your purse strapped across your chest so it cannot be snatched, and carry your credit card and additional cash safe in zipped pockets. Opportunistic street crime happens, but the key is to not be a target and to adopt a few practices that deter criminals from targeting you. It's not rocket science—it's common sense, and we dames have it in spades.

While theft and harassment are two big concerns for women, in Europe theft rarely involves physical violence, and statistically most European cities are much safer than North American ones. *Remember these facts and repeat them while traveling in Europe.* Our apprehension over European destinations is a result of unfamiliarity. The streets, buildings, vehicles, and people are not the same as those in our North American culture, and this

74 GETTING READY TO TAKE FLIGHT

unfamiliarity breeds fear and apprehension. Acknowledging this helps in understanding and rationalizing fears.

Some travel writers (whose target market I suspect is the younger female market) suggest that in order to keep safe, women should not dress provocatively; they are advised to wear an artificial wedding ring, a practice also advocated by some government websites offering safety tips. They also suggest carrying a picture of a husband, real or imagined. I believe common sense is more important than a band of gold and photograph of a man. It is far more important to distribute money and credit cards, so if a purse gets taken, you have backup in your socks/jeans/jacket. Leaving a brief note in your hotel room with the day's planned activities, or emailing a friend about your agenda, is advisable. This means if you do get lost on a long hike and do not return to your hotel, the authorities know where to look. Staying in touch with your family or friends while away is important.

If victimization does occur, try to act philosophically; it happened and there is nothing you can do about it. You cannot turn back the clock. If it warrants a police report, make one; your hotel should be able to provide contact details. If you deem the event too petty, vow it will not affect your holiday. In all my years of traveling, I have been the victim of crime only once. I had my purse stolen in Lisbon when I was traveling alone in my early twenties. I was exploring an area known for crime, but I had not read the guidebook, so I was oblivious. Two young men pulled the bag from my shoulder and ran off. Two police officers were on the scene very quickly to rescue me. They returned me to my hotel, and one stayed to take my statement as the hotel proprietor fussed and gave me brandy, as I was quite shaken. Later that night, the officer returned to ask a couple of additional questions and to see if I was okay. His shift finished, and we sat in the bar and drank port, provided free of charge by the establishment, overseen by the formidable female proprietor who could not speak English but who kept grinning at us both, clearly positioning herself to protect my virtue until the officer left and I went to bed. The event taught me a number of things: be vigilant, always read guidebooks, never carry more than you can afford to lose—but more importantly, although there may be people in the world intent on upsetting you, there are so many, many more who want to make it better, in this case a young, male, English-speaking police officer and an older, female, Portuguese-speaking hotel owner.

⎯⎯→ SUMMARY

Fear of crime is a tremendous barrier to our ambitions. The best way to counter it is to refuse to let it get the better of you. So many times I find myself in a group of women in which someone is recounting a crime victimization story with little objective, it seems, other than to alarm the listeners. Fear is a normal emotion but should not prevent travel. Travel to most international destinations, especially those listed in this book, is no more dangerous than a walk to the local drugstore. Unfortunately our media lead us to believe this is not the case and increase fears of victimization.

In 2014 I went to Prague for the first time and arrived at the main train station. The three guidebooks I had read all stated this was not the place to be. This was the only aspect of my two-week trip to Europe that caused me serious apprehension. I arrived at 6 PM with a vice grip on my possessions and every sense heightened. No one was going to make this girl a victim.

I arrived to find the station full of regular Czech citizens trying to go about their working lives. It was not at all threatening. Numerous single women of every age walked through the station conducting their business. There was even a police office in the station itself. I cursed myself for taking the words of the guidebooks so literally. My heightened fear, while useful, was unfounded. Often after taking a trip you will realize nothing bad happened and will gain confidence. But be warned: inevitably upon return, when telling someone of traveling alone to Chicago, Portland, Amsterdam, or Budapest, they will recount the most gruesome assault they heard about, which happened only last week, and tell you how lucky you were to escape a similar fate. This assault probably happened in Thailand or Brazil, but, from the storyteller's point of view, illustrates why they would never ever leave home without full body armor and in anything other than an impenetrable tank. Listen politely, thank them for their advice, then let them return to Fox News and forget all about it. Pull your shoulders back, hold your head high, and confidently march forward, ready for the next sojourn.

STAYING HEALTHY

It takes more than just a good-looking body. You've got to have the heart and soul to go with it.

—Epictetus

⟶ **INSURANCE**

While I do list basic medical supplies in the "Suggested Packing List" section, there are a few additional things the single woman needs to consider. First and foremost: insurance. Ensure you have good, comprehensive, age-specific insurance, and if you plan to go bungee jumping off the Stratosphere Hotel during a four-day trip to Vegas, make sure the policy covers extreme sports. As I travel a lot, my policy covers all trips I make out of the country up until twenty-eight days and is good for a year. If you plan to travel more than once it is often more economical to get a policy covering a one-year period. Second, if you have any personal issues related to your health, ensure your policy covers them and that you can deal with them while away. The cost of insurance increases as we age, with significant leaps when certain milestones are reached (seventy), so travel while it is affordable (another reason you should stop procrastinating). The amount of insurance purchased and events covered (loss of baggage, trip cancellation, medical, dental, weather extremes, trip interruption/cancellation, etc.) depend on the extent to which you are a nervous traveler. Be sensible and buy what you feel is needed and what you can afford. For example, I always have health insurance, but never baggage, because I feel if I do lose a suitcase, the financial loss will not be devastating. Remember to always read the small print in insurance policies.

——➤ HEALTH

Any medication or routines used at home need to be continued while away. For example, if wearing a knee brace for exercise, pack it—you will probably be walking. If a heat pack is used for aching muscles, take it. (Bags of frozen peas purchased while away make great ice packs if required.) If you take any medication, don't forget it, nor forget to declare it to the insurance provider. It's also a good idea to visit the doctor or dentist, especially if planning to be away more than a couple of weeks and if you've not seen these professionals for a while.

The locations cited in this book do not require inoculations or vaccinations; other destinations may. Still, it's always a good idea to have a tetanus shot. The US Centers for Disease Control and Prevention (www.cdc.gov/travel) has travel-related information on vaccinations for US citizens. In Canada, visit the federal government's Travel and Tourism site (www.travel.gc.ca).

When away, there are a few simple things you can do (or avoid) to keep healthy:

- Drink bottled water.
- Do not pet dogs or other animals, no matter how cute. (The same may also be said for the opposite sex.)
- Wash hands often.
- Take anti-nausea pills if traveling long distances on local transportation.
- If in need of a doctor, ask the hotel to contact an English-speaking one.
- Be cautious of food from street vendors and use good judgment in all food establishments.
- Carry a small first aid kit (sting relief, Band-Aids, insect repellent, ibuprofen, pain medication, sunscreen, antiseptic cream).
- The most cited illness that affects travelers is diarrhea, commonly caused by bacteria in food and water. Bring medication from home and keep it in your first aid kit; if you become ill in the middle of the night, treatment is close at hand.
- Drink plenty of water during a flight.
- Remember to get up every two hours on a long flight and stretch. On transatlantic flights I usually walk to the back of the plane to stretch, use the restroom, and chat to other passengers. A number of exercises can be completed while seated in a plane such as shoulder shrugs, back stretches, ankle rotations, and head rolls. All help.

- Carry antibacterial hand gel—the bathrooms in even the most developed countries sometimes leave a lot to be desired.
- Exercise. This will probably occur through walking, but if you are not accustomed to walking eight hours a day, your holiday will not magically impart this ability. Consider increasing physical fitness prior to departure.
- Get enough sleep. It's far better to see a new place well rested than tired. When you're weary, problems are more likely to occur.
- If engaging in sexual activity (or planning to), always use a condom.
- Constipation (or "total shutdown" as my friends call it) is a common complaint by women visiting foreign lands, so consider purchasing something to counteract this state before you leave home.

⟶ JET LAG

For many, jet lag—officially named desynchronosis (who knew?)—is a real issue, especially if you travel across multiple time zones. Unfortunately no one has really solved the problem. Various supplements like melatonin may help; you may also want to try aromatherapy oils such as lavender, bergamot, and neroli, but I must admit I've not tried these. My advice is to skip the pills and potions and try to adjust to the new time zone as soon as possible. Some travelers try to adapt to the new time days in advance, but this can be difficult. Being well rested before a long flight helps. When traveling to Europe I set my watch nine hours in advance of Pacific Standard Time the moment I get on the plane. Suddenly 6 PM becomes 3 AM. When I arrive, I try to stay awake until 8 PM, which is very difficult but imperative to make the most of my time away. Being outside and in daylight helps to get over the time difference. *Do not nap.* Napping, even for an hour, is disastrous. I usually find my first night of sleep is fine, and I wake early, which is good. The second night is more difficult, so it's a good time to go to bed with an extra glass of wine. I often do find myself wide awake at 3 AM, but when that happens, I don't get up, or read, or watch TV; instead I recall the words of my mother: "Even if you're not asleep, at least you're lying down and resting." Do set an alarm—it's easy to oversleep as the body adjusts. When returning from Europe to North America, try to arrange travel for a Saturday (often the cheapest day to travel) so Sunday can be the recovery day.

Of course, jet lag can be alleviated by some shut-eye on the flight. But while I *can* rest on a plane, it's very difficult to sleep. Earplugs, neck pillows, and blankets help, as does wearing comfortable clothes and removing shoes. If sleeping is a priority for you, book a window seat to avoid being disturbed. The best travel books (and the medical profession) suggest avoiding alcohol when flying, but I find drinking two glasses of wine—as long as they are consumed with copious amounts of water—helps me relax. (After the age of fifty it becomes easier to avoid advice that's good for you). Continue to keep hydrated once you arrive at your destination.

When away, make it a top priority to get enough rest; being alone *and* tired can be very unpleasant. Although time on holiday is precious, it is far better to be mentally and physically alert—and it's preferable to limit excursions rather than be completely exhausted, trying to cram everything in. Tired individuals are also more vulnerable to crime and victimization.

Be rested so you can appreciate the new culture. It's a holiday—
look after yourself!

→ MENSTRUATION TO MENOPAUSE

Before menopause, the first thing I calculated before booking
a trip was not the cost, the emotional impact on my children,
or the clothes I needed—it was the probability of having my
period when away. For this avid female traveler, the joy of not
packing tampons is as good as getting an engagement ring
from George Clooney. When the monthly bleeding stopped
I gained a new appreciation for what a pain menstruation
is to the traveling woman. Menstruation can be embarrass-
ing, not only for those experiencing it, but for those around
them. During one of my first trips to North America I found
myself in the restroom at the back of a Greyhound bus in New
Jersey. I was sitting on the toilet, balancing a wrapped tampon
on my knee when suddenly the bus jerked; the cylindrical
device fell to the floor and rolled under the locked restroom
door and into the corridor of the bus, where it continued
to roll around for my entire three-hour journey, and maybe
beyond. The journey was tense. Just when I thought this wad
of cellophane-wrapped cotton had made its last appearance
(perhaps wedged under a seat or stuck in an air vent), it
would reappear, content to entertain the bored passengers
as it danced around the moving vehicle. Of course I, and my
fellow passengers, tried to ignore it, but as luck would have it,
a six-year-old boy (whose mother had failed to bring anything
to entertain him on this journey) asked in a loud voice if
he could go and pick up the white tube. When denied the
opportunity, the child then gave an articulate, full account of

the tampon's location, velocity, and direction. This three-hour journey took a lifetime to complete. Is it any wonder I love my post-menopausal, non-bleeding body?

If you are still in this phase of life, pack sanitary supplies—you never know when they will be needed. Although all international destinations do carry supplies, sometimes the instructions are not clear. I once purchased a well-known international brand of tampons in Italy only to find they were suitable only for menstruating elephants. The color code "pink" used in North America for medium-size tampons did not translate in Italy. In Italy, the instructions on the pink packet obviously stated these tampons were suitable only for large, Catholic, Italian women who had experienced natural childbirth on ten or more occasions. These tampons were colossal, and I didn't realize the size until the early hours of the morning when circumstances demanded the box be opened. The tampon's diameter required a bleary eyed, half-awake woman in a richly tiled, mirrored Italian hotel bathroom to slice the much-needed item in two using the only device at hand: curved nail scissors. At such times one questions whether any other woman has ever experienced the same set of circumstances, and why the makers of this sanitary wear (men?) would choose different color codes for different countries. Lesson learned!

And while you're thinking about packing the appropriate supplies, make sure to include any medication used at home for menstrual cramps, headaches, or any other conditions. If you do need a pharmacist, ask your hotel to recommend one. It's not unusual for menstrual cycles to be disrupted or delayed because of travel, so be prepared, not alarmed, if this occurs. Remember contraception, as you never know who you may meet, to prevent pregnancy and protect against the various sexually transmitted diseases. Holiday romances do not just happen to teenage girls, and even though they may not be on your agenda, a condom weighs nothing.

→ RESTROOMS

This brings us to what is arguably the most important subject in this book, a topic near and dear to my heart—and one that most guidebooks skim over or fail to address: where to pee and poo. When I was younger this was not such a big issue—I could go for ages without the need of a restroom. But at my age, and after two kids, this is no longer an option. If you find a nice clean loo, use it, even if you don't feel the need—you never know when the next opportunity will present itself. This is particularly true for European cities, especially early on in the vacation when you have not yet become familiar with the new city. In my lifetime I have probably wasted a week of valuable holiday time wandering around cities in search of clean restrooms. On a positive note, these excursions have introduced me to some interesting places not in Fodor's guidebook, most recently in an old established hotel in Santa Fe, where I had to resist taking a "selfie" because the tiling was so good.

The location of restrooms is far more convenient in North America (with perhaps the exception of New York) than it is in Europe, as most North American department stores, restaurants, and museums are well equipped and facilities have been built in the last hundred years. This is not the case in Europe. A few years ago I attended the musical *Chicago* in London's West End. The theater was over two hundred years old, as were the three stalls in the ladies restroom. The flushing system was also the same age, so once the toilet was flushed, the cistern would take five minutes to refill. A lot of women wanted to pee during the fifteen-minute intermission. This involved lining up and out of the restroom along the stairs towards the bar and waiting until one of the three toilets was vacated. This experience was recently repeated at the Budapest Opera house, a fantastic building over one hundred years old, but again with few loos. Be prepared. The Broadway hit musical *Urinetown* was conceived and written by a composer who, while traveling on a limited budget through Europe, sometimes had to decide whether to eat or pay to use the toilet. This is no joke, especially to the mature woman. Some large department stores in England require visitors to purchase something there before allowing them to use the facilities (the code for entrance to the lavatory is printed on the receipt). The Starbucks coffee bars in Prague also have this policy. In Italy, small cafés have restrooms for both men and women; France is notoriously short on providing loos; a number of European train stations demand payment and the correct coins to enter, but then the cubicles are not large enough to accommodate the client and her large suitcase. I once found myself in the small market town of Ilkley in England and wanting to go. The turnstile entrance to the public restroom accepted only twenty pence pieces, a coin I did not have. As it was early evening, not many people were around and options for peeing were few. After consideration, I found myself contorting and squeezing my body under the metal barrier to gain access without payment. For the rest of the holiday I was sure my deviance had been caught on closed-circuit television, and I wondered if I would be arrested for unlawful peeing in an English market town.

Despite this depressing picture, the peeing/pooing issue can be addressed when traveling. Most museums and art galleries grant visitors access without requiring them to pay for entrance, so you do not have to actually visit the gallery to "spend a penny." Visitor centers often have facilities (or can direct you to them), as do town halls and government buildings. Larger hotels with bars and restaurants open to non-residents always have restrooms in their reception area, normally clearly signposted. Walk with confidence into the Hilton, Hyatt, Sheraton, or another high-end hotel and look for them, or ask at reception. Usually, no one denies access to a conventionally dressed "woman of a certain age" and the facilities are generally good. In Europe, make sure you always have tissues on hand; toilet tissue in the cubicle is often a prized commodity (especially later in the day or during the peak summer tourist months). When you pack your stash of tissues, slip a small bottle of hand sanitizer in your purse.

Some Eastern European cities have paid toilets, usually policed by large, dour-faced women dressed in white, demanding a stated sum or proffering a "tip plate." After depositing coins in the plate, customers are granted access and provided with three sheets of single-ply toilet tissue. I have yet to see any of these women smile, but I suppose this is not surprising given the nature of the work. Despite the grim "customer service" and the scant amount of toilet tissue given, the facilities are well kept.

→ SUMMARY

Few things are worse than being ill away from home, but if it occurs, accept it, take medication, and hunker down. Look after yourself to ensure the speediest recovery. This is where the importance of pre-trip preparation and planning proves itself: In 2015 I was due to take a long trip and broke a toe six weeks prior to my departure. I could have returned to exercise classes after four weeks, but chose not to as I wanted to be completely recovered and fit for the excursion. I substituted swimming for high-impact step classes and so maintained a healthy body but did not apply additional stress to the vulnerable parts. The best body to take away is a fit and healthy one, so try to ensure your body (and mind) is in the best possible shape. Make sure you are well rested, eat well prior to departure, and maybe cut down on alcohol consumption if you know (like I do) that one of the treats of being away is that extra glass of wine. Looking after your body before you depart will enhance your enjoyment of your trip.

A number of governments issue warnings about health, political stability, and safety for every country, and regularly update this information on their websites. See www.travel.state .gov (USA) and www.voyage.gc.ca (Canada).

MONEY SMARTS

Travel is the only thing you buy that makes you richer.
—Author unknown

⟶ **DEAR READER (AND NOW I** really sound like Jane Austen, not Jayne Seagrave): Although I am oblivious to your financial status, I presume you have money to travel or can obtain it. As we get older, we find we have accumulated a lot of "stuff." Sure, our clothes still fit (albeit tightly); we have twenty-five or more pairs of shoes; our home is furnished, our children are educated, our jewelry box is crammed full, and our mortgage is small or non-existent. What we lack, however, is a full treasure chest of adventure stories, which we can fill up only by actively seeking out and collecting experiences. This is why I allocate my "spare" money to travel. It's not money wasted—it's an investment. And it's not just an investment in ourselves: my mother is almost eighty, and I've given up buying her birthday or Christmas gifts. Instead, I visit her and give her experiences and events she can then tell her friends about while adding to her own treasure chest of memories. My first three-month solo adventure was when I was eighteen, working in a summer camp for two months in New York State, traveling on $400 for the remaining four weeks. I carried only cash—no credit cards. In my last four days I had $20 left. Even now, after thirty years, I cannot get over the power of the credit card and the fact I own one. This little piece of plastic means if disaster strikes and all my luggage is lost, the hotel loses my reservation, the airline rejects my booking, or I have to return home quickly, I can do so; I can pay. This is the reality of being older and is another real advantage of maturity. What kind of financial security and backup do you have? Do you have a contingency plan that not only takes care of your needs at home, but also gives you a guaranteed way out in case of emergency when traveling? If not, what can you do to secure this?

--->COSTING IT OUT

When considering solo travel, you must first decide on how much to spend. If you live in New York and have a budget of, say, $2,000, a weeklong trip to Rome is out—but you can have a comfortable week in Savannah and stay at a nice hotel without scrimping. As mentioned earlier, when considering where to travel, start small and local, and then increase the length of the trip away, both geographically and time-wise.

Almost without exception, most travel writers and

guidebooks orient their information to the younger student traveler, and while there is nothing wrong with hostels and one-star hotels on the edge of town with shared restrooms, my raison d'etre is to encourage mature women to travel, hopefully with a certain level of comfort. My advice would therefore be to stay somewhere safe, clean, adequately heated and/or air conditioned, quiet, and comfortable. Stop somewhere you want to stay. Part of the enjoyment of travel is relaxing in a decent hotel room with all comforts. Aim to wake up in a bedroom that's more luxurious and furnished to a higher standard than you're accustomed to, or is at the very least as comfortable. I recently had a trip to a small Scottish town where the Best Western hotel was $200 a night, but a smaller two-star establishment had awesome views of the sea at half the price. The bed in this hotel, although small, was comfortable, and the furnishings were old but fully functional. As I intended to spend very little time in the room, I made the wise choice of staying at the two-star. I saved money and did not suffer as a result.

Assess how much the hotels and flights will cost by using websites such as Expedia and Travelocity. Key into the search engine different months to determine pricing at different times of the year. Some locations (e.g., Prague, Edinburgh) are cold, damp, and dark during the off-season (November–March) but are much less crowded with easier to find, considerably cheaper accommodations. Shoulder seasons (April–June, September–October) are often the most desirable times because of warm (not hot) temperatures, the absence of schoolchildren, and accommodations/flight savings. Summer (high season) can be unbearably hot in certain areas. Consider the pros and cons on the basis of your agenda and commitments. My favorite time to travel to a city tends to be the off-season (despite the fact it can be cold and gets dark at 4 PM) because of the lack of crowds.

To reiterate my earlier point: include an emergency fund for unanticipated expenses, and if on returning home it has not been touched, put the cash toward the next vacation. A few years ago I arrived in Charlotte, North Carolina, ready to rent a car for my sixty-kilometer trip to meet a customer, only to find my driving license had expired and the option of renting was not available. My hotel suggested they arrange a car and driver for me. The next morning, I was met by Errol and his gleaming white Cadillac with large, deep, black leather seats and polished wooden dashboard. Both the vehicle and man sported the subtle aroma of pine mingled with aftershave. Errol was tall, fit, and well dressed, and spoke in a charming southern drawl. He and his vehicle were more expensive than the car rental agency, but meeting him meant I did not have to navigate unfamiliar roads, get lost, or stress about traffic and arriving at the appointment on time. He suggested routes that introduced me to North Carolina scenery and large plantation architecture I would not have found myself, while supplying interesting anecdotes as my tour guide and driver—an unintended consequence and an additional expense, but, to quote a well-known credit card company, "priceless." Had I rented a car, there's no doubt the trip would have been deleted from my memory. I will never forget Errol.

Guidebooks on the targeted destination often have costing for hotels, museums, attractions, tours, etc. that provide a good idea of how much is needed. Remember, most financial information is out of date the moment it's published, so be sure to determine when the book was released; similarly, web-based data is reliable only if it has been recently updated. Keep in mind when costing out potential activities that many of the best tourist sights can be free (museums, cathedrals, churches, parks and gardens) or have free days/evenings. In any case, it's always better to over-budget than to be shocked by the expenses upon arrival. Inevitably, payment will be needed for something you do not anticipate (e.g., lost cell phone charger, diarrhea medication with English language instructions, taxi fares). The larger, most popular cities (London, Paris, New York, Chicago) tend to be the most expensive.

In creating a rough itinerary of where to go, where to stay, and what to see, you'll get a general sense for whether it fits your allocated budget. If it does not, question whether you can modify by traveling in the low season, visiting for a shorter period of time, or staying in a different, less expensive hotel, for example. If it doesn't fit into your budget, consider alternative locations.

⟶ FINANCIAL PRACTICALITIES

Take a small amount of the local currency, enough to cover two to three days, so upon arrival there is cash for taxi fares, airport food, tips, etc. Order this currency from a bank and try to receive it in small denomination notes, as no one wants to change large bills. Look at and play with these notes to become acquainted with them; by doing this there is less chance of being given incorrect change during a transaction.

Remember to tell your credit card provider where and when you will be traveling, as sometimes card providers put a stop on a credit card when unfamiliar activity occurs on it. Ensure your credit limit is sufficient to cover expenses you expect to incur. I rely heavily on Visa cards and take local currency from local ATMs. Without exception these ATMs have instructions in English. Never take large quantities of cash from these machines and, if possible, use the ones located in banks or hotels. Each time you use one you will have to pay a fee, but that is better than walking around with large sums of money. ATMs dispense money in local currency and give better exchange rates than hotel receptions or exchange offices. Keep all receipts. Never exchange money on the street or with strangers—the risk is not worth it, no matter how attractive the street exchange rate is, or how cute the individual offering this service appears.

While tipping is an established North American practice, it is not so readily undertaken in European countries and is a culturally specific custom. Guidebooks detail local practices. I like bringing the North American habit of tipping abroad, as showing appreciation of the individuals working in the service industry is frequently justified.

Make copies of your passport, which should be current for at least six months after the travel date and tickets, and if you've paid in advance for accommodations, take a copy of the credit card statement showing this. Always book flights or accommodations using a credit card; if something goes wrong a request can be made to the credit card company to reverse the charge. I travel with a number of envelopes inside a larger envelope and label them as follows: photos of docs, accommodations, flights, car rental, expenses, etc. to give some order to this information. This envelope is kept with my passport. You can also keep copies on your cell phone.

Before traveling, empty your wallet of the cards you will not need (library, social insurance, department store loyalty cards).

Remember, photographic identification is required to board a flight, so if you don't have a passport, make sure to carry other documentation.

Arranging financial information and determining if your dream trip is affordable are part of the planning process. These activities should not be a chore—they are vital because, when you're away, it's disconcerting to discover that a must-do activity (such as visiting the Tower of London) or personal necessity (three cappuccinos per day) is prohibitively expensive. Doing research before you leave home will save you money. For example, when booking a hotel in England, you might learn that the establishment you're considering charges £20 a night for parking, but by undertaking a quick online search of car parks, find that parking in an adjacent privately owned one costs only £10. Traveling within an established budget, sticking to this financial commitment, and being aware of the costs associated with visiting the location are vital to avoid monetary surprises during the holiday.

OTHER WAYS TO TAKE FLIGHT

Twenty years from now you will be more disappointed by
the things you didn't do than by the ones you did do. So
throw off bowlines, sail away from the safe harbor. Catch
the trade winds in sails. Explore. Dream. Discover.

—Mark Twain

⟶ **JUST AS THERE ARE AN** unlimited number of destinations
women can travel to alone, (and in the next half of this book, I
suggest twenty-three cities that are fabulous places to visit on
your own), there are also alternative methods and styles in which
to travel. The following is a brief synopsis of these and includes
road trips, organized tours, cruises, and packaged vacations.

⟶ **ROAD TRIPS**

The quintessential girl-power moment comes when a lady takes
to the open road alone for an extended period of time. Nothing

can compare with the freedom this engenders. In celebration of my fiftieth birthday I embarked on a five-hour road trip between Las Vegas and the Grand Canyon before descending to the bottom of this geological wonder on a mule. In my zippy little red rental car, I crossed the arid, dusty scenery on an almost-deserted highway, singing loudly to the music playing on a "Hits of the Eighties" radio station. Thelma and Louise without Louise—total self-indulgent freedom. I adore road trips because I love driving, and this is the key. Road trips are ingrained in my psyche and are a lot more common for North Americans than for people of other nationalities. In Europe, because of the excellent train system, trains are the preferred method of transportation, whereas in poorer economies with weak infrastructures, bus transportation is often the only option. In North America the road trip is king, and for the most part services exist for North American residents and guests to indulge in this passion.

Anyone who is a nervous driver, dislikes being in total control, or hates unpredictability should reject the idea outright. Road trips for the single woman are attractive for a number of reasons:

- They can be taken directly from home (no flight/train or additional expense).
- They can be as long or as short as required—two days, two weeks, two months.
- They can be spontaneous and unplanned—wake up and go.
- They require less organization and planning than other vacations.
- They tend to be more economical than city-center-based holidays.

- They acquaint and educate the driver of the broader geography of a country, state, or province.
- They are a safe way to see the world.
- Luggage or overpacking is not an issue as a lot can be packed into a car.
- They can be added onto an excursion. For example, you can fly to Denver and drive to Santa Fe, or leave home and drive to Las Vegas.

When undertaking a road trip, two options are available: start from home, or catch a flight, rent a car, and explore another destination. Leaving from home is easier because of familiarity with the vehicle and the country. Once the departure decision is made, another choice has to be made: How much prior planning should you undertake? You can map out detailed itineraries by calculating driving distances, listing locations to be visited, booking accommodations, and researching every detail. Google Maps provides information on routes, distances, and driving times. This option ensures there is a destination at the end of each day to aim for. Alternatively there is the "wing-it" option—have a rough idea where to go and stay, and take every day as it comes in a totally unplanned manner. Numerous travel guides have detailed road trip itineraries. The books I write on camping in British Columbia offer seven, fourteen, and twenty-one day road trip ideas. State and provincial government tourism bodies often provide suggestions for the driver, including points of interest at which to stop. These are great for clarifying your ambitions and helping you make decisions about where to go and for how long. Agencies such as AAA and CAA also have good data. Road trips are good for getting a bigger picture—taking in scenery and geography rather than buildings and cities.

I have taken solo road trips in Newfoundland, Alberta, British Columbia, Ontario, Yukon, England, Scotland, and to a number of US states. I tend not to book accommodations in advance; instead I always have a general idea of where to stay, and I travel with hard-copy accommodations guides, because as Internet connections in some areas may be poor. With wheels, accommodations on the edge of town are often cheaper, and cruising around to select something visually appealing is possible, especially if you're looking during the shoulder seasons. However, with a decent Wi-Fi connection, booking accommodations in the morning when the evening destination is known is a safe option. Although my preference is to book in advance, a couple of years ago I found myself at 8 PM looking for accommodations in the relatively small town of Wainwright, Alberta. I knew there were numerous hotels, but what I did not know was that the Royal Canadian Mounted Police (RCMP) Musical Ride was in town and, despite it being a Monday night in early September, everywhere was full of Mounties and their adoring fans. I eventually found an old, badly lit motel on the very edge of town. I was the only female guest. The functional establishment was oriented to men working in the oil and construction industries; there was a large fridge in the room for my beer, a huge space in the car park to accommodate my truck, and a tin can outside my room for spent cigarette butts. My small room, with its nylon bedspread, smelled of chlorine and was devoid of tea- or coffee-making equipment, of fluffy white towels and a thick cotton duvet—but it did provide a hair dryer, circa 1950. Everyone left noisily at dawn and I followed suit. From this I learned to plan and commit in advance if there is a remote chance that accommodations in the destination could get fully booked.

Driving and navigating strange cities, especially at the end of the day, can be challenging. Smaller communities may also have limited dinner/food options after 6 PM. I arrived at a small Newfoundland town once and booked into the only motel. There was no gas station or store open. The vending machine in the hotel was broken and the restaurant closed (no demand on a Tuesday night). My dinner consisted of instant oatmeal and red wine—the only food in the suitcase. Booking in advance also has the advantage of forcing a stop. Sometimes on road trips it gets to about 5 PM and you have to decide whether to drive on and stop much later, or stop prematurely. I have frequently made the mistake of driving on and then regretted the decision as night fell and hours passed before I found another hotel.

Long hours of driving make arms/backs/legs/bums ache, and can make you less alert, so it's important to get out of the car frequently to walk and stretch, even if your surroundings aren't particularly compelling. When I stop I try to select rest areas where there are at least three or four other cars and basic bathroom facilities. I'm cautious about stopping in deserted locations or where there is only one other vehicle (unless carrying a family). I have greater fear in these locations than I do in cities. While street smarts are needed in cities, "single smarts" are needed in remote, roadside locations. Of course, if the scenery is stunning, there is nothing to prevent a driver stopping anywhere and remaining in the car for a rest and refreshment break.

During my road trip across Newfoundland there were few alternatives for coffee, Wi-Fi, and restrooms, so I got to know one chain of donut shops very well, as these were the only option in most small communities. While the scenery was fantastic, the choice of refreshments wasn't. This is often the disadvantage of travel in unpopulated areas where gas stations provide the only respite. Of course, you can break up long road trips by extended stays in towns and cities, which add variety to the driving.

Driving a well-maintained, reliable car is important, and the condition of the vehicle should not be an issue if it's a rental. Before you even get in the vehicle, make sure all the tires are inflated, and have on hand AAA/CAA insurance, a GPS, a working cell phone and charger, a good road map, a bottle of water and some snacks. When on the road watch the gas tank, especially if crossing long distances with few communities. I try to keep the tank half full, as nothing is worse than seeing the gas tank light come on indicating you're low on fuel, especially when you're driving an unfamiliar rental car—you won't know how long it will be before the vehicle stutters to a stop, or where the next gas station is, if indeed there is one. When parking for the night, try to do so under a bright street lamp and as near as possible to the door of the accommodations. Finally (and returning yet again to my favorite subject), some gas station restrooms on the open road are not good places to sit and read the latest edition of *Vogue*; fast-food restaurants are preferable, and in many small towns you can find McDonalds. Though not a fan of the company's culture or cuisine, I am an absolute devotee of its restrooms and the clean, hygienic service this chain provides for the woman on the road who wants to pee.

I find road trips are the loneliest method of solo travel, as everything is constantly new. Even when you're alone, if staying in a location for a number of days, the hotel environment and staff become familiar after a few days. And being in an urban environment necessitates communication and listening to others—again, even if you're by yourself—as you interact with taxi drivers and ticket agents for buses, metros, and trains. Driving alone to different locations, for the most part, prevents this from happening. Road trips are exhilarating, fueling you with an adrenalin rush as you meet each unscheduled day, because *anything* is possible. Being the one behind the steering wheel offers the greatest sense of empowerment and independence, and the car becomes a private venue for unhindered, unselfconscious karaoke. Packing a few drinks and snacks for unplanned picnics by the side of the road in locations you'll only ever visit once—and will probably never find again—will make for some delightful memories.

In summary, one of the greatest joys of taking a road trip is being the sole navigator while encountering unpredictability. Turn a corner and be gobsmacked by snow-capped mountains; discover a little Bavarian-themed town that no tourist book has found significant enough to detail; find yourself on the famous Route 66 when you least expect it; stumble upon the perfect artisanal ice cream shop when craving a sugar burst; or take shelter at a small, cozy pub because the road ahead is flooded and will not be cleared for twelve hours. Road trips grant both adventure and a safe freedom for the mature woman as you hit the open road, cocooned from the elements in the comfort of your warm, dry car. So pack your bags, fuel up the car, and choose your favorite sing-along tunes—this holiday will be one entirely unique to you.

Before I say anything else, I must admit I have taken part in a few organized tours and generally dislike the structure. I know myself—I do not want to pay a fee to be told what to do or where to go with people I perhaps do not like and don't want to spend time with (and who probably don't want to spend time with me). When I see tour guides waving umbrellas, flags, and hats on poles at groups of bored, tired-looking, unenthusiastic individuals wearing name badges as they shuffle at a snail's pace behind their leader, I want to run, vigorously shake them all, and convert them to solo independent travel. While part of me is delighted my fellow human beings are out exploring the world, another part questions the mode employed. Tours frequently require insulated interaction with a group from your own country, social class, and ethnic origin and prevent true immersion in another location or a foreign land. While undoubtedly safe, many tours do not offer more than the slightest exposure to a different culture, and it is for this reason I am not a fan.

With that rant out of the way, let me enthusiastically acknowledge organized tours do offer a safe environment for the single woman. I readily believe tours fill a gap and provide a needed service. Tours exist for almost any destination and for virtually every length of time, and may focus on specific interests (e.g., art history in Italy, cooking in France, spas in California, wine tasting in Australia, sailing in Greece) or on a specific country or region. They can be booked through large tour organizations (e.g., Intrepid Travel www.intrepidtravel. com and Contiki www.contiki.com) or though generic websites such as www.flightcentre.com. Small companies specializing in customized tours to specific countries or interests can be

found—for example, for those who want to explore India (www
.indiaodysseytours.com), or those who love photography (www
.photoworkshopadventures.com).

The number of tour operators has increased tremendously
over the last twenty years as the word "tour" has been replaced
with "trip," "vacation," or "adventure," perhaps to move away
from the negative and dated connotation of the four-letter
word "tour."

The real advantage of tours for single women can be in the
access they grant to non-Western cultures (e.g., India, Asia,
China, Africa), which present greater challenges for the solo
traveler. The cities and countries recommended in the following
pages have cultures, food, standards of hygiene, and economies
similar to our own; although clean restrooms with flushing
toilets may be hard to find in Barcelona or Dubrovnik, they
exist and just need to be hunted down. Some areas of the world
are particularly challenging because they are so unlike our own
and have different values, customs, and sanitary and hygiene
standards. The languages are tricky or seemingly impossible
to understand, and the accommodations and transportation
systems confusing, unstructured, and crowded. Organized tours
provide everyone access to these cultures and in this respect
should be applauded.

Travel literature has identified certain types of tours as more
attractive to the solo traveler, such as yoga retreats, volunteer
vacations, outdoor adventure, and language programs. Some
tour operators specialize in the solo market and advertise
accordingly (e.g., www.adventuresforsingles.com, www
.solotravel.org, www.allsinglestravel.com). All are at pains to
stress they are not dating agencies. Having never been on one

of these tours, I would say the key to enjoying this mode of travel is to know yourself—are you tolerant of others and their idiosyncrasies and habits? Can you withstand these, or do they annoy you? Remember, the cheaper the tour, the younger the clientele; some tours have age restrictions.

A number of tour companies target single women and make it clear that kids, husbands, or partners are not permitted. (www .thelmaandlouise.com, www.gutsywomentravel.com, www .adventuresingoodcompany.com, www.TodaysWomanTraveller .com). These organizations offer to take groups of women to every corner of the earth, often for "female activities" such as spa treatments and shopping excursions, although many also offer adventure packages or general cultural trips.

In summary, if deciding to commit to any kind of tour, ask yourself the following questions:

- Is the itinerary acceptable (e.g., is there too much walking or too much eating, is there enough time to see everything you want, does it go where you want to go)?
- How much time is given in each location? Is this sufficient?
- What are the sleeping arrangements and class/ratings of the establishments?
- What is the size of the group? (Tour groups generally consist of between ten and forty people.)
- Who else is going—singles, families? What is the gender and age breakdown?
- Are you able to adjust to living within a group and dealing with the personalities of people in it? What will you do if an obnoxious, needy traveler is in your group? Can you cope or will the holiday be ruined?

- What is the cost? (Tours can work out to be considerably more expensive than planning a trip by yourself.)
- Do any of the excursions require specific equipment? If so, is there an additional charge?
- How much time is spent traveling between destinations? What is the mode of transportation?
- How much free time is allocated?
- If the tour is canceled, will you be compensated? (Check the small print—some tours are canceled if they don't attract enough participants.)
- How long has the tour company been in business?
- What is the ratio of tour leaders to participants? How experienced are the guides?

To supplement my scant knowledge of organized tours, I recently attended a presentation by an established Canadian women's tour group. There were about twenty women in the room, all of us between the ages of fifty and seventy. One woman loudly blew her nose for the last twenty minutes of the presentation; another asked the same question on five separate occasions. If either of these two individuals had been on a tour with me, I would have been arrested for committing some unspeakable violent act! I am not a tour gal, but am quick to acknowledge that tours can provide a safe environment for the novice. And if the goal is to meet new people *and* explore new places, organized tours are ideal and should not be ignored.

——> CRUISING

Each year the cruise ship industry grows; latest figures suggest it is worth over $30 billion. I have taken two cruises and believe they offer everyone, including the single woman, a safe, secure, sanitized, and sometimes cost-effective way to travel. For those who have never traveled alone, cruises help take the novice from dipping a toe into international waters to diving into more ambitious adventures. I took my first ten-day Alaskan cruise with my family over eight years ago; before we boarded the colossal ship I was dreading it because of all the clichés about overeating, overweight, and over-age participants. Instead it was a wonderful, stress-free experience. I did not have to think for myself for the entire duration—everything was taken care of. More recently, I took a short repositioning cruise from Los Angeles to Vancouver at a cost of $200 (which included three nights, two days, and all food; the two-hour Air Canada flight between the same destinations was $157 plus $25 for checked luggage—and no food). What's not to like?

With over thirty thousand worldwide cruises to choose from, everyone should be able to find something appealing. At first blush, cruises seem to provide excellent value for your money, at times working out to be under $50 per person per day; that said, there are a number of additional expenses, not least of which are single-person supplements, which can be as much as 200 percent, making some of these advertised bargains not so attractive to the single woman. The cruise companies make their money by numerous add-ons, charging for shore excursions, most non-alcoholic, alcoholic, and specialized drinks, gambling, Internet access, and some recreational activities—and there is a mandatory daily fee for staff services. (The key access card to your room acts as an on-board credit card.)

Traveling by ship grants the opportunity to visit more than

one place (albeit briefly); food is provided twenty-four hours a day, seven days a week, in a variety of restaurants; pleasant accommodations and restrooms reflecting North American standards are offered; evening and daytime entertainment is available; and numerous recreational and shopping activities are at your fingertips. Cruises are easy to book through conventional websites such as Expedia or Travelocity. (In terms of flying to and from port, many cruise ship companies advise booking with a travel agent.) Ships can accommodate many thousands of people or just a few hundred. River cruising in Europe has grown in popularity, with the capacity of many vessels being under three hundred. Many believe cruising is just for the elderly, but recent data indicate that the average age of first-time cruisers is under forty. In addition, over 25 percent of cruise passengers are single (over four million a year). To reflect this, some cruise lines are adding single rooms to their fleets and have singles meet-and-greet events. Even so, single cabins are rare, so single supplements are the norm.

An extensive library of travel literature exists on every aspect of cruising (e.g., cruising with kids, cruising for singles, first-time cruising, European cruises, river cruises), as well as online information and blogs. In addition, a number of travel agencies devote themselves to this market, aware that many people take only this type of holiday. (If interested, take a look at www.cruiseshipcenters.com.)

The downside to cruising is similar to that of the organized tour discussed above: embarkation takes place with many thousands of others; disembarkation is regimented and can take considerable time, so six hours on shore erodes to four; ports get crowded (especially in the Caribbean where multiple ships dock at the same time, each with over 2,000 passengers); additional expenses mount up easily. There are also considerable environmental considerations. And while cruises offer a taste of travel, they rarely provide an in-depth experience of the city in which they're docked. The allotted time passengers have to explore is limited—and the brief time on land is often shared with other passengers. Cruise companies make money when passengers are on board, not off.

In summary, cruising provides a safe and stress-free way to travel, but no excitement or adrenalin rush. The single cruising woman is not her own person. And for the most part, cruises do not allow participants to do more than scratch the surface of the country visited. For the nervous single woman a cruise can be a useful first step, but after this initial excursion, I'd encourage her to take a more serious foray into a different culture without the crutch of the cruise crowd.

ALL-INCLUSIVE PACKAGED VACATIONS

I have never taken a prepackaged vacation alone, but with my family I've taken over twenty to Cuba, the Caribbean, Mexico, Costa Rica, Spain, and Morocco. Indeed, many resorts want to attract couples and families and so aim their advertising at them. While in many ways ideal for couples or families, such vacations are much less appealing for the single woman, primarily because in many North American or Caribbean hotels, escaping the hotel complex is difficult—unless you rent a car or take an excursion, which tends to be with the aforementioned couples and families. For the solo gal who wants to sit by a pool, read numerous books, work on her tan, not think about anything, and is comfortable with eating alone in large buffet restaurants full of happy revelers, such resorts could be just fine.

Packaged vacations (like cruises and tours) need little planning and forethought. I recently read one guide that described them as a land-based cruise. There certainly are similarities: once booked, everything is included—flights, transfers, accommodations, sometimes all food, and often all alcohol, as well as entertainment and sports activities. While leaving the hotel to explore is possible, many package tour destinations easily reached from North America are not that welcoming (or safe) for single women because of where they are located. This is not the case for many packaged tours from Europe. And remember, the single-room supplement can ramp up the costs.

Some packaged vacations offer the choice of the "European plan" (breakfast only) or an "almost inclusive" option (no lunch). These alternatives require the participant to find lunch and/or dinner themselves by paying an additional fee at the hotel or leaving the hotel and finding local restaurants. Websites such as Expedia and Travelocity have great search engines for potential clients to choose established packaged vacations (e.g., those provided by companies such as Sunwing, Air Canada Vacations, and Virgin) and compare prices and departure dates. These sites also allow customers to build a custom package by combining their hotel and flight. Such an alternative may be more economical, but it also means running a gauntlet of taxi drivers upon arrival at the destination and figuring out which one will most reliably and safely deliver you from the airport to the hotel. This is anything but a stress-free experience for the first-time female traveler arriving in countries such as Mexico or

Costa Rica. Finally, the price of this type of holiday can increase considerably once the single-room supplement is applied.

⟶ SUMMARY

All these alternatives—road trips, organized tours, cruises, and packaged holidays—offer the single woman a number of ways to take flight, and with the exception of independent road trips, they are really, really structured and safe. And they extend the already huge range of options available.

WHY I RECOMMEND THE
FOLLOWING DESTINATIONS

The world is a book, and those who do not travel read
only one page.

—Saint Augustine

⟶ **THE FOLLOWING SECTIONS DESCRIBE ELEVEN** North
American and twelve European cities that single women
can visit safely and easily. The cities included have spawned
a great deal of travel literature describing accommodations
options, restaurant recommendations, and the places visitors
must see. In addition, websites, magazines, travel programs,
and government agencies have added to and duplicated this
extensive literature. My aim is not to reproduce this, so I make
no specific recommendations about hotels or restaurants.
And although I do list a number of must-see sights, my

recommendations are meant only as a guide and are based on personal experience. My primary objective is to give advice to encourage women to take flight by suggesting destinations that, through my own travels, I have found to be interesting, safe, and female friendly.

In this digital age we are overrun with information. I wrote *Time to Take Flight* in the belief that what women with a passion to travel want is not another guidebook or website listing a hundred museums, two hundred hotels, and three hundred restaurants; this information already exists. What you want is a gender-specific synopsis of cities suitable for your individual needs. This information serves as a springboard from which you can make informed decisions. Consult more comprehensive, site-specific works to find additional facts. On the basis of my travel experience, I focus attention on four aspects that I deem important to the single female traveler:

- *Reasons to recommend the city:* This often includes safety and security issues, restrooms, and costs, and takes into consideration the city's notoriety and popularity as a tourist destination.

- *Access from the airport to the city center:* I've often found this to be the most challenging issue when traveling as a single woman, and one often overlooked in literature.

- *Desirable neighborhoods (and areas within the city itself) with good accommodations:* Many cities are extremely large, so selecting a safe hotel that also affords easy access to the destination is vital for the enjoyment of a vacation.

- *Recommended activities suitable for the single woman:* In addition to describing some of the activities I've enjoyed first-hand, I include online resources to assist with your own planning.

The choice of cities and information in the following pages is based on my own experiences, tastes, and preferences. I've visited each location at least once (Dubrovnik, Savannah, Prague), many on numerous occasions (Chicago, Las Vegas, Paris) and some I have lived in for a number of years (London, Vancouver). There are, of course, a number of other cities that could have been included but have not been listed.

For the most part, the recommendations made in the following pages about destinations can be adapted to accommodate the reader's age, socioeconomic status, geographical location, physical and mental health, relationship status, confidence, prior travel experience (either solo or with others), and personal travel preferences.

I received no financial remuneration or gratuities from any of the cities, companies, and organizations mentioned. Unlike many travel writers who receive incentives from hotels, tourism departments, and cities to publish positive reviews, I have chosen not to pursue this path. The decision to look at these specific locations was completely my own. While I have included the costs of some services (such as transportation), these are approximations influenced by exchange rates and subject to yearly increases. Use them only as planning guidelines, and do some research on the Internet if you want current information.

The North American and European cities are listed from largest to smallest, but other than by size are in no order. I do not have any favorites; all have their own individual charms and attractions. My advice is to try to visit them all.

The ball is now in your court; you are the only person who can choose. While my intention has been to offer guidance and support, at the end of the day (and at the end of the book) the choice to take flight is entirely yours. My hope is that in five, fifteen, or even fifty years from now, when the mind and body are slower and reflection is the order of the day, you will a full treasure chest overflowing with delightful memories—and absolutely no regrets for travel opportunities missed. *Carpe diem!*

TIME TO TAKE FLIGHT
IN NORTH AMERICA

NEW YORK

Take Flight for

DIVERSITY
MUSEUMS
TRANSPORTATION

I go to Paris, I go to London, I go to Rome, and I always say there's no place like New York. It's the most exciting city in the world now. That's the way it is. That's it.

—Robert de Niro

⟶ **AS THE FIRST NORTH AMERICAN** city I journeyed to by myself at age eighteen, New York holds a special place within my solo travel affections. With limited finances during my first night in North America, I stayed in a very seedy, but centrally located, hotel. At that time, New York suffered from a poor reputation. It was run down, neglected, and crime ridden. I recently performed an Internet search to find out if the hotel was still in existence. It is—complete with a litany of online complaints about bed bugs. While the quality of this hotel seems not to have improved over the last thirty years, the same cannot be said for the overall city itself. During subsequent visits I have been impressed with how the Big Apple has cleaned up its act. New York improves year by year: it's cleaner, more polite, and much less threatening than it was when I first encountered it. Reported crime is lower than it has been for years. So it is now the perfect place for the street-smart single woman to visit.

But this single babe needs money, as New York is anything but cheap. With so many things on a "to-do" list, this girl also requires energy and a precise agenda to make sure she gets the maximum benefit. The city attracts over fifty-five million visitors a year—not surprising when you examine what's offered. World-renowned architecture such as the Empire State Building, Rockefeller Center, and Statue of Liberty compete for precious time with internationally acclaimed galleries such as the Metropolitan Museum of Modern Art and the Guggenheim. Areas like Greenwich Village, Times Square, and Central Park call for attention, as do the Brooklyn Bridge, Wall Street, and hundreds of theatrical productions both on and off Broadway. And don't even get me started on the shopping. Any excursion to this wonderful city requires detailed planning, energy, and an acceptance that if all goes according to plan, another visit will be required in the not-too-distant future.

──→ ARRIVAL

Three airports serve New York City. The main one is John F. Kennedy, where the AirTrain links to the city's subway line for a journey downtown, which takes about an hour and costs $5. An express bus ($16) and shared shuttle vans go to Manhattan hotels ($25), and taxis run at about $50, excluding tolls and tips. LaGuardia Airport may be closer to the city but is not well connected; the best option is to take a cab (approx. $50) into town. Newark Liberty International Airport has trains running to New York Penn Station ($12), express buses ($16), shared vans ($25), and taxis ($60–$80). Penn Station is the arrival point for Amtrak and provides easy subway connections, while buses arrive at Port Authority Bus Terminal—the world's busiest bus station with over seventy million passengers a year—from where subway trains depart. Needless to say, all transportation hubs are very busy.

—> ACCOMMODATIONS

The most popular time to visit is in the summer, which is when prices increase as well as temperatures. The best time to stay in New York is the spring or autumn, as the winters can be bitterly cold. Over the years, many large chain hotels have established themselves and can provide "bargains," but these bargains may still be expensive. The average rate of hotel accommodations was over $300 a night in 2015, but with some serious research, securing a room around for $200 in a three-star hotel is possible. Guidebooks such as those in the Fodor's and Lonely Planet series divide the city into neighborhoods, list the advantages and disadvantages of each area, and have suggestions, so research using these and travel websites such as Expedia. Times Square, Midtown, and the West Side offer better deals. Bed and breakfasts and furnished apartments are also an option. The choice is staggering. Weekdays tend to be cheaper than weekends, and last-minute bargains can be had if you are prepared to wait and take a risk.

I cannot stress enough the need for targeted pre-trip research and planning for the woman who wants to get the most out of this busy metropolis. For the first-time visitor, the list of possibilities is truly endless. Make detailed itineraries on the basis of the time you have, priorities, and locations. Divide the city up according to the number of days available and then target the attractions in that area to factor in food breaks and looking for restrooms. Restrooms are not easy to find, so remember when you see one to visit it. Also plan for a number of unintended events—unplanned excursions will inevitably arise and add to the color of the journey. Consider purchasing a travel card, which entitles you to seven days of unlimited travel for $30, and a CityPass, which offers discounts at a number of venues such as the Empire State Building (open until midnight), Museum of Modern Art, and Ellis Island. While walking is a great way to see the city, the 660-mile subway system is a safe (as long as you use the usual street smarts), cheap ($2.50 per ride), sweaty (in the summer), dirty (but it *is* a hundred years old) alternative. Be aware that the subway gets very crowded during the morning and evening rush hours. Then there is the shopping, the skyline, and neighborhoods (Greenwich Village, Chinatown, SoHo, etc.). Plan, plan, plan!

⎯⎯➤ ADDITIONAL INFORMATION

If you hate noise and avoid crowds, you won't like New York. If cleanliness and order are high on your agenda, research alternatives. If you want a place to be at peace with the world and connect with your inner Zen self, know that New York is not that place. While locals and visitors complain about traffic, congestion, noise, and crowds, New York City continues to be very much *the* place to be. So if you want to see magnificent works of art by some of the great masters, take in award-winning theater, explore alternative arts, eat designer food or revolutionary street cuisine, and visit iconic locations, plan a visit now. New York is constantly changing; as a vibrant city it should be on everyone's bucket list—just don't expect it to be a relaxing holiday. And as far as safety is concerned, you'll be pleased to know the crime rate has decreased since the early eighties. In 2014 there were 333 murders in the city; in 1984 there were 1,384. Violent crime has decreased by 51 percent since 1991. There has been a greening of the city, and bikes are everywhere. Now that I'm in my fifties, New York is a friendlier and more open place than when I was in my teens and twenties. I'm confident you'll find it a friendly and open place too.

——> **WEBSITES**

newyorkhotels.com
newyorkpass.com
nycgo.com
nycvisit.com

CHICAGO

Take Flight for

ARCHITECTURE
SHOPPING
RIVER CRUISES

Eventually I think Chicago will be the most beautiful great city left in the world.

—Frank Lloyd Wright

⟶ **I'VE VISITED CHICAGO ABOUT FIVE** times in the last ten years, primarily for trade shows. The shopping is fantastic—and that's saying something since I am not really a shopper. On my most recent visit I vowed not to be drawn into the retail haze and was determined instead to spend more time on the cultural and historical aspects of the city. Harboring self-righteous intentions, I took the self-guided historical walking tour, only to be led to the lobby of the flagship Macy's store. What's a girl to do? My tour information instructed me to gaze up at the Tiffany vaulted ceiling, visit the fountain, experience and indulge in The

Walnut Room, the first restaurant ever established in a department store. I was completely taken with the edifice but also became distracted. It was March, and all winter attire had been reduced by 70 percent. Once I caught wind of this, staring at the ceiling and fountain could not compete with such seductive retail bargains. (Anne Klein soft leather jackets were on sale for under $100!) I did eventually finish the walking tour, but it took way longer than originally planned.

You could easily spend a week or more in this city of nearly three million people. The skyline and skyscrapers ringing the Lake Michigan shoreline, the elevated subway lines, the waterfront parks packed with joggers, and the sheer mass of population all contribute to the city's unique energy and edge. This is not a calm, relaxing venue for a solo girl trip. The city screams, "Do this, do that, come here, go there!" as the noisy trains clatter overhead. There's a gritty edge to America's third-largest city, and it's not shy to parade its industrial (and Irish) roots. With over forty-four million tourists a year, Chicago emanates optimism and swagger, confident all visitors will be impressed.

—→ **ARRIVAL**

O'Hare International—located seventeen miles out of town— is the city's main airport, one of the busiest in the world. My impression is that it seems more like a bus terminus than an airport; everyone seems to be rushing, there are not enough seats for the multitude of travelers, and fast-food outlets (not designer retail outlets) dominate O'Hare. And, amusing as it sounds, the restrooms are well worth a visit—check out the toilet seat protector; in all my travels this is something

I have only encountered at O'Hare. I'm sure most visitors spend an additional two minutes in the cubicle playing with this unique device, which automatically engulfs the seat with plastic wrap. But I digress. From the huge airport, a $5 ride on the CTA Blue Line takes about forty minutes to the downtown Loop and runs twenty-four hours a day, seven days a week. Shuttle vans are by far the better option for the single dame, operate to individual hotels, take about an hour, and cost $32. Taxis are around $50 and take from thirty minutes to over an hour. If arriving at Midway Airport, the same three options are available with the CTA Orange Line costing $3, airport shuttle $27, and taxi around $40. Amtrak has more connections here than anywhere else in the USA at the beautifully restored Union Station and is centrally located, as is the Greyhound bus station, although both places are not welcoming at night.

———▸ ACCOMMODATIONS

Chicago is home to a number of huge trade shows and conventions, so many big hotels—centrally located near the Loop—cater to these clients and other customers. More recently, trendy "designer" boutique hotels have grown up in outlying areas such as Wicker Park, where it is also possible to find bed and breakfasts. Stay as central as you can, because as some of the outlying areas can seem a little threatening, as can taking transit at night. Hotels on or just off Michigan Avenue, if your budget extends that far, are the most desirable. Chicago is a big city, so use your street smarts no matter where your hotel is located.

You can get a good sense for most of the cities included in this book after visiting for about three days, but Chicago is an exception; three days in this metropolis barely scratches the surface. There's so much to do—where to start? I strongly advise taking the self-guided walking tour, details of which can be obtained from the Chicago Visitor Center (77 E. Randolph Street), located in a great building. This tour will provide an introduction to the Loop, which houses a high concentration of historical buildings as well as the Art Institute of Chicago and the Willis Tower, with incredible views. I had a fantastic night overlooking the city while consuming Blue Lagoon cocktails on the 96th floor lounge; there I spent the same amount of money I would have had I gone to the very top of the tower, yet I still enjoyed the same awesome view. As mentioned above, if you get distracted (which is very easy in Chicago) the Loop Walking Tour can take all day. I also recommend taking a river cruise; many such tours bill themselves as architectural tours, and from the water visitors are shown a diverse array of magnificent buildings key to the industrial development of the city. Chicago's most visited attraction is Navy Pier, which has a number of small touristy stores, restaurants, and attractions (check out the stained-glass-window museum). And, of course, no visit would be complete without a stroll along Michigan Avenue—specifically the Magnificent Mile and Macy's, the second-largest department store in the world.

$\longrightarrow$ ADDITIONAL INFORMATION

Chicago is not known as "the Windy City" for nothing. Timing a visit will have a huge influence on what you can and cannot do.

Travel bargains can be had from November to March because the weather is so damn cold, but really this is a city that needs to be seen between April and October. While serious crime has been falling, the city has a definite edge. Crimes of opportunity, such as pick-pocketing and cell phone theft, are an issue. When I visited (and despite staying in the touristy areas) I had occasion to feel apprehensive when out during the early evening; some areas adjacent to the Loop may give rise to an uneasy feeling, even in the daytime. While this in no way should prevent a visit, Chicago is a big North American city; take precautions when visiting it. In summary, Chicago is a big city with tons to do—and even more to buy.

——> **WEBSITES**
chicagotraveler.com
choosechicago.com
cnscvb.com

BOSTON

Take Flight for

HISTORY
ICE CREAM
WALKING TOURS

Boston was a great city to grow up in, and probably still is. We were surrounded by two very important elements: academia and the arts.

—Leonard Nimoy

⟶ **MY FAVORITE FOOD (AFTER RED** wine—is that a food?) is ice cream. The highest consumption of ice cream in the USA is in Boston, with an average of twenty-six pints per person per year. For the woman who loves ice cream, a visit to Boston is a total no-brainer. The single girl with the sweet tooth must research this part of Boston culture, especially since the *New York Times* recognized the Boston store Toscanini's (www.tosci .com) as having the best ice cream in the world. Yes, I should be focusing on the breathtaking architecture, Harvard (America's oldest institution of higher learning), the wonderful waterfront

setting, the vibrant arts scene, and Boston's significant historical importance in the development of the USA (with more sites
detailing aspects of the American Revolution than any other
city). But really, can't all these cultural and historical attractions be experienced in between and during the consumption
of ice cream?

Boston is the oldest city in the USA; the moment you step
out of your hotel you will encounter architecturally significant
buildings, walk on narrow cobbled streets, and be immersed
in history. For anyone who loves history (and ice cream—did
I mention ice cream?), Boston should be high on the agenda.
In addition, Boston is a relatively small, compact city with
most of the attractions within a one-mile-wide, three-mile-
long area, making it easy to navigate. Getting lost should not
be a problem—and if you do get lost, it will be among some
wonderful buildings.

───> ARRIVAL

Getting to the center of Boston is a breeze. Boston's Logan
International Airport is relatively close to the center of town
and accessible by the T subway line (the oldest in the USA)
for a fare of $2; alternatively, you could take a taxi ($25–$30).
The city is also well served by Amtrak and Greyhound, from
which connections can be made to the T subway.

───> ACCOMMODATIONS

As a big city with an active conference, academic, and tourism
scene, demand for accommodations can be high, so book early.
The most desirable areas are Beacon Hill and Boston Common,
but these are also the most expensive, as they have the added

advantage of being centrally located. The downtown core is also good but may be a little noisy for some. A little farther out, the communities of Back Bay and Kenmore Square offer a neighborhood ambiance. Avoid accommodations in the South End and Chinatown—those areas have a poor reputation and can be dangerous. When I was looking for accommodations a few years ago, a hotel website warned visitors to avoid the adjacent areas at night, so when booking make sure you research the location well.

→ ACTIVITIES

After thirty years of solo travel, I don't know why more cities have not followed Boston's lead by painting a red line on their sidewalks indicating a walking tour of the main sights for tourists to follow. During my first-ever visit to Boston, about fifteen years ago, I took the Freedom Trail and followed this line. It was during my early days of traveling alone, so I was still a little nervous about exploring. I deeply appreciated the person in the Boston Department of Tourism who developed the red-lined walking tour. When I followed this line, there was no getting lost, no looking at complicated maps, no wondering if I was at the right junction—there was simply no confusion. This was a solo traveler's dream and, for a single woman not known for her cartographic expertise, a real bonus. The Freedom Trail, a two-and-a-half-mile, well-marked route, introduces the tourist to all the main historical sights. It leads from Boston Common to Bunker Hill, but ensures the follower stops at significant points such as the wonderful Faneuil Hall and adjacent Quincy Market. The Beacon Hill area has cobblestone streets and brick townhouses that create a gorgeous atmosphere for quiet contemplation. By straying from the red line even more is discovered. There is also a Woman's Heritage Trail and a Black Heritage Trail. Any woman can spend days following these trails and encountering Boston's fascinating historical past. A visit to Boston is not complete without a trip to Harvard, which offers free tours of the campus, and the adjacent quaint neighborhood of Cambridge, with its coffee shops, restaurants, bookstores, and gift shops—and where street performers congregate in the summer. Obtain a good map and walk along the water's edge of the Charles River, where the university rowing crews practice, or take a boat tour. Whale watching tours take place from the harbor.

> ADDITIONAL INFORMATION

Although Boston is the tenth-largest US city, it does not feel large. Being relatively compact it is ideal for the woman who wants to learn of US history in a slow, methodical way, taking routes originally laid out as cow paths and consequently forming no regular pattern. The best time to visit is in the spring when the cherry blossoms are out. Boston has been described as "the Athens of America" because of the architecture and vibrant arts scene. Many of the museums and galleries have been upgraded in recent years. If your intention is to visit these cultural establishments as well as the other wonderful buildings, and if you want to take full advantage of the ice cream culture, plan to spend more than a few days. As long as exploration takes place in the central areas, the city is safe for the solo woman, but some areas in the vicinity are not so accommodating.

⟶ **WEBSITES**

bostonusa.com

cambridgeusa.com

cityofboston.com

massvacation.com

SAN FRANCISCO

Take Flight for

ALL-SEASON ACCESS
ALTERNATIVE CULTURE
ICONS

Anyone who doesn't have a great time in San Francisco is pretty much dead to me.

—Anthony Bourdain

⟶ **EVERY TIME I ARRIVE IN** San Francisco I have an immediate sense of déjà vu. Thanks to the media, we've already seen the iconic streetcars, Golden Gate Bridge, steep hills, and brightly painted houses in hundreds of films and TV shows. But there is a huge difference between a digital portrayal and the in-person experience. During my visits I found the hills steeper, the bridge less red, the houses brighter, and the streetcars noisier. Seeing San Francisco in a movie cannot compare or even come close to being there. Films are great for inspiring us to take action and commit to exploration, but the excitement of actually seeing an icon is priceless. The joy of the city for me is that it can be appreciated at any time of the year (unlike, for example, Montreal, New York, or Chicago, which are difficult to navigate in winter, or Las Vegas and Santa Fe, which can be too hot in the summer). It is not as large as Chicago nor as small as Portland, and has a reputation for being the home of hippies, alternative culture, and a cosmopolitan arts and culture scene. The forty-seven hills spread out over seven square miles provide a good workout for even the fittest gal, and the welcoming coffee bar culture is well entrenched, so there are a multitude of options for refreshing tired limbs.

──➤ ARRIVAL

Two international airports serve San Francisco. If arriving at San Francisco International Airport, an easy option to downtown is the BART non-stop train (with a fare of approximately $8). For a better alternative, try the shuttle buses, which deliver the traveler to the door of their hotel for about $20. Taxis run at about $40. If arriving at Oakland International Airport, you can take the BART, but the required changes are in some seedy locations, so it's preferable to take a cab, especially if arriving at night—however, these can be expensive (around $60). The city is served by Amtrak and Greyhound, but both stations are away from the downtown core, so if arriving by bus or train, you'll need to take the BART or a taxi.

──➤ ACCOMMODATIONS

Now for the bad news: San Francisco is not a cheap city to visit and accommodations rates are high. The most reasonable rates can be found off-season and during the shoulder season months of January–March and October–November—but be warned: during conventions the city can sell out of accommodations. With that in mind, sometimes weekend rates can be better bargains as the business community vacates. Choose accommodations within the Marina/Fisherman's Wharf or Downtown Civic Center areas. Both areas are touristy and safe, are close to the main attractions, and have a number of chain hotels. I last stayed in the Wharf area and enjoyed the vibrant street scene during the day and early evening. The North Beach, Chinatown (which can be noisy at night), Hills, and Japantown areas are all good, cheaper alternatives, but are a little farther out; however, they offer more boutique accommodations and bed and breakfasts. For the affluent dame, Nob Hill is the location for luxury and really good views of the city. Because some areas of town are unsavory, check reviews before booking, especially hotels with bargain rates; single women should not consider staying in certain locations.

→ ATTRACTIONS

As a criminologist (albeit lapsed), I loved the cliché tour to Alcatraz, which you need to book in advance if it's on your bucket list. The trip takes the better part of three to four hours, but the history is fascinating and it's an iconic experience. The cable car rides are also quintessentially San Franciscan and will take you through a number of the city's distinct areas, offering a good way to identify regions (and coffee shops) for subsequent investigation. Chinatown is a small compact neighborhood worthy of exploration, as are the other areas of Nob Hill, Russian Hill, Telegraph Hill (go see Coit Tower),

Union Square (for shopping) and, for a complete contrast, the Financial District.

The lady with energy should take a day to walk from Fisherman's Wharf to Golden Gate Park. On Saturday there is a market on the wharf, and on every day of the week look for the sea lions (but be prepared for the smell, which the tourist literature does not stress) along the waterfront. When I took this day's hike, Girl Guides of America was having a national jamboree; thousands of girls and their leaders were everywhere, adding even more color to the city. As I've said before, these unplanned encounters always lead to further enjoyment and memories.

Although walking everywhere is possible, the transportation system is excellent. Food carts and cafés are prolific, and for the cultural visitor, the Museum of Modern Art is a must-see.

→ ADDITIONAL INFORMATION

The Golden Gate Bridge is one of the most photographed structures in the world, so isn't it time to go beyond the images and see it yourself? Absolutely, but when planning to do so, remember that San Francisco is often hidden in a blanket of fog. One of the issues in visiting this city is the weather. Summer is often the wettest, dampest, windiest time. Tourism literature often quotes Mark Twain, who stated that the coldest winter he ever experienced was a summer in San Francisco. September is probably the ideal time to go, but with mild temperatures throughout the year, the choice is open as long as you pack thoughtfully. My times in San Francisco have been characterized by taking off and putting on clothing, so before leaving the hotel in the morning, choose clothes for every eventuality. Lightweight, breathable layering is a good strategy.

Despite hosting almost sixteen million visitors a year, San Francisco does not feel too crowded. And as home to the gay and lesbian revolution, it has a great sense of tolerance and is a friendly, inclusive, accommodating city. Finally, for the female traveler, it is quite safe as long as you take the same precautions you would in any other large North American city.

———> **WEBSITES**

baycityguide.com
sanfrancisco.travel
visitsfbayarea.com

MONTREAL

Take Flight for

INTERNATIONAL FLAVOR
STREET SCENE
ACCOMMODATIONS

Montreal, this wonderful town . . . pearl of Canada, pearl of the world.

—Mikhail Gorbachev

⟶ **FEEL LIKE VISITING FRANCE WITHOUT** crossing the Atlantic? Then how about a trip to Montreal, "the Paris of the North," for a true alternative culture? This four-hundred-year-old Canadian city on the banks of the St. Lawrence River packs a pretty big punch and is an exciting metropolis with a population of almost two million. Famous for poutine (fries with cheese curds and gravy), patisseries, and smoked meats and bagels, as well as numerous cafés and restaurants, this city has a unique and safe street scene. It has more food choices per capita than any other city in North America (with the exception of New York) and has a true bohemian feel. Add to this an extensive lineup of festivals and events, a historical district of cobblestone streets, a vibrant arts community, first-rate shopping and parks, and the stage is set for any dame to have a full, diverse agenda during her stay. Montreal is not an expensive place to visit; accommodations are plentiful and available in every price range. There is a good transport system, eating out is very reasonable (compared to the costs in other large North American cities), and the crime rate (based on criminal code infractions) has decreased by 37 percent since 1991, making it a very safe, attractive large city for the single girl. With all this, what's not to like? Well, unfortunately the winters can be really brutal, so Montreal is not a year-round destination.

⟶ ARRIVAL

If arriving by air at Pierre Elliott Trudeau Airport (formally Dorval) the cheapest way to the center of Montreal is by bus and metro ($8). Bus 747 outside the arrivals hall takes you to Gare d'Autocars, which links to the metro (also called the STM, which stands for Société de transport de Montréal). But be warned— this journey can take over an hour. Alternatively, a taxi costs about $50, depending on traffic, which can be heavy. Several hotels have shuttle bus services that can be a real money saver. Amtrak has a service between New York and Montreal; it takes eleven hours and is slow, but the scenery is terrific. Greyhound and VIA Rail offer services for travel between Canadian cities.

⟶ ACCOMMODATIONS

Montreal has a vast array of accommodations options suitable for every style and budget, from designer chic boutique hotels, to historical bed and breakfast establishments, to large chain hotels, to university accommodations (over the summer months) that offer well-priced, self-catering, and private room sleeping arrangements within easy walking distance of Montreal's attractions. Although not super cheap, accommodations rates tend to be a lot more reasonable in Montreal than in many other North American cities such as New York or Chicago. Old Montreal has the most historical, though frequently more expensive, accommodations, but if the budget stretches that far, go for it (be warned, though: the area can be noisy at night). Alternatively, choose accommodations in the Latin Quarter, which is semi-residential but has numerous tree-lined streets and an array of bars and cafés. I really liked the ambiance of this neighborhood, and consequently I prefer staying there. The Plateau/Mont-Royal area is also good, but a little farther away from the main sights. However, the metro is easily accessible, so even if you stay in this area, you will easily be able to take the public transit to a number of tourist attractions.

⟶ ACTIVITIES

Montreal is a great city to cycle around, and unlike many other cities that have introduced bike-share programs with a lukewarm reception, Montreal's program, called BIXI, has been a great success with both tourists and locals—and rightly so as it's easy to navigate. A number of downtown streets have designated bike lanes.

The joy of Montreal is not only the food but also the French culture. There is a distinctly different feel about the place. Anyone with three days to explore can pack their time by concentrating for the first day on the area around Old Montreal (and the revitalized Old Port area), with its winding cobblestone streets, shops, and clock tower; then, hike to the top of Parc du Mont Royal for wonderful views of the city. Day two can be spent exploring the neighborhoods of Little Italy, Plateau/Mont-Royal, and the Latin Quarter. Finally, spend a day shopping in the downtown core on Ste. Catherine Street West, meandering along to see McGill University and perhaps the historical Westmount region, which contains some of the most expensive property in Canada and where a number of historical homes can be viewed. This itinerary, of course, does not include excursions to the city's many museums and galleries and open-air markets, so you may consider a longer trip—perhaps a week or more if you're ambitious; there's certainly plenty to see in a week to ten days. If you want to explore the outer reaches of the city, the clean, safe metro system makes such trips quite easy; you may wish to visit the site of Expo 67, now a park, or the Montreal Biodome, which features replicas of South American, North American, local, and polar ecosystems.

⟶ ADDITIONAL INFORMATION

The best time to visit is undoubtedly the summer, despite the high humidity. Winter here can be really harsh, as mentioned earlier, and as I believe a lot of the enjoyment of the city is on the street, the severe negative temperatures means a winter visit will restrict activities (and remember, spring can be delayed, sometimes not arriving until May). Be sure to keep this in mind when planning your trip.

Although French is the predominant language, everyone in the service industries speaks English. Montreal is Canada's arts and cultural capital and home to the world-famous Cirque du Soleil. Throughout the year—especially in the summer—you can find a variety of festivals, the most famous being the Montreal International Jazz Festival. Taking place at the end of June and attracting nearly two million visitors, this musical extravaganza happens every day for twelve days, from noon until the early hours. Accommodations prices increase during this period as they do for other events such as the popular Grand Prix. If your passions involve the arts, and not necessarily the mainstream theater productions found on Broadway or in London's West End, consider a trip to Montreal.

———> WEBSITES

montreal.bixi.com

montreal.qc.ca

stm.info/en

tourism-montreal.org

LAS VEGAS

Take Flight for

VALUE
PEOPLE WATCHING
NIGHTLIFE

Las Vegas is a twenty-four-hour city. It never stops.
—Eli Roth

⟶ **WHEN THINKING OF THE IDEAL** destination for the mature, single female traveler, Las Vegas may not be the first destination that springs to mind, but it should be. Over the last ten years I have attended about fifteen trade shows and conventions in this city and have developed a quirky fascination for the place. I love it for the tackiness, the people watching, the ease of arrival and departure, and its non-threatening nature. Vegas is not full of young, beautiful people, just regular, relaxed folks on holiday. And you don't have to be a gambler to enjoy Vegas, which someone once described to me as being "Disneyland for adults." Nor do you have to stay at the expensive designer hotels or dress up to the nines.

Vegas is a people place—a very welcoming *mature* people's place. The city provides easy access to lovely hotel pools (which are somewhat noisy but far enough away from gamblers), easy, reliable, clean transportation, two great outlet malls and countless shopping opportunities, unlimited opportunities for observation of local and visiting characters, spectacular shows, street performers, day trips, tours, and more. Even with all that, it's not an expensive city to visit, especially if you search for bargains and choose the right time of year. Vegas should be on every travelers' to-do list, even if only once. In 2014 Vegas had just over forty-one million visitors. Everyone who visits has an experience and flies home with a story. It's a city full of constantly changing personalities. Visitors return home either saying "never again" or eagerly planning the next trip.

Vegas is safe for mature, female, single travelers because there are so many mature, single, female holidaymakers there—safety in numbers. It's also the destination for a multitude of conventions and trade shows, so unlike many other holiday destinations where the single traveler is an anomaly, in Vegas it's almost the norm, as so many are in the city to attend a work-related event. Every time I visit, I make a point of taking in a show and usually find I'm seated next to another single person who is also in town for a show or convention. After this treat I walk the Strip and am thoroughly entertained by the vast array of people of every age and ethnic origin doing exactly the same.

⟶ ARRIVAL

The airport is quite close to the city, and arriving in Vegas by air is a delight (unless you get in after 11 PM or depart before 7 AM, as the shuttle is not available during those times). Getting from the airport to your hotel—presuming it's on the Strip—is a brief $8–$11 shuttle bus trip away. What other location in the western world can make this claim? A number of companies operate shuttle bus services to drop visitors at their hotel doors, picking up from outside the baggage claim area where tickets can be purchased from clearly marked kiosks. While on these buses, inevitable conversations start up; if you're lucky enough to be the last passenger dropped off, you will also get a glimpse of where everyone else on the bus is staying and hear recommendations from fellow travelers on where to go and what to do (or not do). Shuttle buses, often driven by colorful characters, return to the airport but require booking in advance. There are, of course, taxis, but they're considerably more expensive, especially if they get stuck in evening traffic, which can be really, really heavy. Amtrak does not have a service to Vegas, but you can reach the city by Greyhound bus.

⟶ ACCOMMODATIONS

Tens of thousands of hotel bedrooms offer accommodations in every price range, but anyone arriving for their first time *must* stay on the Strip to be near the action. The older hotels are located at the northern end of the Strip (e.g., Circus Circus, Stratosphere), offer the best prices, and are perfectly adequate, although they provide somewhat dated accommodations. Each year it seems another new hotel more dazzling than the previous one opens its doors. Be aware that prices increase when large trade shows are in town, as well as sports events, during holidays, and over the weekend. Still, rates can be very reasonable during the week, as there are so many rooms on offer; prices do fluctuate considerably. A first-time visitor should not stay in Old Vegas, as this is away from the Strip, but should make a point of visiting.

———> ACTIVITIES

For me there are four must-do activities: take the Deuce bus, walk the Strip, visit the outlet malls, see Old Vegas. While this is the place for good walking shoes, take the Deuce bus upon your arrival, sit on the upper deck (at the very front if possible), and stare out at the hotels to establish the lay of the land. Once this arduous task has been undertaken, determine which attractions and hotels to return to for further exploration on foot—the Eiffel Tower at Paris, the Sphinx at the Luxor, or the gondolas at the Venetian. There is a wealth of possibilities. Each hotel has food courts, designer restaurants, coffee shops, gelato cafés, bars, and, of course, gambling. Be warned that when exploring it is very easy to get lost within the subtly lit hotel itself. The Deuce runs up and down the Strip, and for $8 offers an unlimited on/off passport for twenty-four hours, $20 for three days. During the evening, walking between stops is frequently quicker than taking this bus, as the traffic can be bad and the loading/unloading time consuming. Walking the Strip is safe, as so many tourists are doing the same. Men peddling cards for call girls and prostitutes come out around midday, stand at street corners, and stay until the early hours. While this activity seems remarkably pointless and annoying, you can easily ignore it; in my experience these men do not target women. Elvis impersonators, mime artists, painted live statues, and

Disney characters add to the colorful street scene. Tickets for shows can be bought from hotels or from a number of vendors (e.g., the Fashion Show Mall). There are two shopping outlet centers, with one at either end of the Strip and accessible by the Deuce. These are ideal if the temperatures get too hot and air conditioning is required. Fremont Street is the "old" Vegas and also can be reached by the Deuce. For travelers wanting to go farther afield, trips to the Hoover Dam and Grand Canyon are readily available.

→ ADDITIONAL INFORMATION

Vegas puts everyone in a good mood, and even those of us who travel primarily for work to "Sin City" cannot help but feel its pulse and energy. Everyone seems to be on holiday and having fun, but if you get offended by seeing endless pictures of scantily clad women (and men) displaying the curvy body you never had even when you were their age, Vegas may be a step too far. One surprising thing in the twenty-first century is how smoking is permitted in the casinos and in some public areas of hotels. While the newer hotels have excellent ventilation, for me the presence of cigarette smoke is one of the biggest drawbacks. I usually visit Vegas in early May and even at this time it can get really hot; carry water or buy it from the numerous ABC stores (which are also good for sushi and snacks if you decide after a day of exploring to return to your room, put on your pj's, watch a movie, drink wine, and eat in bed). Vegas is in the desert; I do not know how anyone could enjoy the city in the forty-degree heat of July and August, so when planning a trip think about the time you want to go. It's becoming a go-to place for bachelorette (and bachelor) parties, so it's easy to encounter groups of women dominating the sidewalks while wearing similar clothes. Finally, when wandering, stay in well-lit areas to avoid any possibilities of opportunistic crime, leave your expensive jewelry at home, and wear comfortable clothes and shoes to appreciate it all. Choose Vegas if undecided on which North American city to experience solo for the first time. Even if you never return, everyone should visit at least once—it's a totally unique experience.

———→ WEBSITES

lasvegas.com

vegastourism.com

visitlasvegas.com

PORTLAND

Take Flight for

ACCOMMODATIONS
WALKING
BOOKS

Portland in particular is a cheap enough place to live that you can still develop your passion—painting, writing, music. People here seem less status-conscious.

—Chuck Palahniuk

———> **IN AUGUST 2014 I SUGGESTED** to my family a four-day trip to Portland. I had visited on previous occasions and liked the size, culture, and funkiness of the city and wanted to take an eight-hour train trip from Vancouver to introduce the city to my offspring. My two teenage boys did not think hanging around a city in mid-August with their mother was going to be fun. "There's nothing to stop you going by yourself," they said. And they were right—there was nothing to stop me. After a seven-hour Amtrak train ride, much of which was beside the Pacific Ocean, I arrived at the wood-paneled Portland Railway

Station, one of the oldest in the USA, at 2:30 PM; I walked fifteen minutes to my hotel to deposit my belongings, and by 3:15 PM was lost in the sun-drenched downtown streets. An Italian festival was taking place on the main square, so after a few hours of exploring and reacquainting myself with the city's core, I sat in the early summer evening's heat at Courthouse Square. There I consumed a slice of pizza and a glass of wine in the open air, listened to an eclectic collection of music, including folk, opera, and contemporary rock, and watched people of every age and ethnic origin dancing. It was fantastic, free entertainment—and, for me, totally unplanned. I can't say it enough: one of the greatest joys and understated benefits of travel are these unanticipated events. You can see Portland, Oregon, in three days; a number of distinct neighborhoods make it attractive. Outdoor markets, reclaimed industrial zones, quaint suburban residential streets, parks, and the Willamette River all add to its glory, as do the prevalence of food trucks, coffee bars, craft breweries, bakeries, and restaurants. If food is your thing, Portland is for you. The cultural and arts scene here is vibrant, and the shopping is not bad, either—and all within an easy-to-explore compact area.

───> ARRIVAL

Portland International Airport (PDX) is located about thirty minutes from downtown by taxi (approximately $40 depending on traffic). Alternatively, for under $3, take the Max Red line from the baggage claim area to Pioneer Square. This must be one of the easiest journeys from an airport to a city center anywhere in North America. The Amtrak train and adjacent Greyhound bus station are within easy walking distance from downtown, and although at first sight the route to the center of town may seem threatening, I don't think it's any more threatening than many other destinations—as long as you arrive in daylight. A taxi from the train station to a downtown hotel is not expensive; definitely take one after dark or at any time of the day, if you feel at all uncomfortable in this environment.

——➤ ACCOMMODATIONS

A wealth of hotels, motels, and bed and breakfasts is available to choose from; prices vary depending on the location, star rating, and time of year. Many independent hotels offer quaint services/facilities (afternoon tea, local craft beers, works of art for sale, libraries, funky breakfast buffets, reduced rates for those in the performance arts) or are themed (wine country, French salons, classic films, avant-garde), and are located in older buildings, adding to the overall character. Spend time not only locating the right hotel, but reading about the decor and architecture to take full advantage of your time away. If your budget allows, choose one of these full-of-character buildings— you won't regret the investment.

——➤ ATTRACTIONS

One of the highlights of visiting Portland is the diverse array of neighborhoods, all which you can visit easily by meandering at a comfortable pace. Exploring does not demand traveling for miles or using transit; the city is nicely compact and easily explored on foot. Historical buildings, as well as trendy shops and eateries, are all closely packed in the central downtown/ Pioneer Courthouse Square area and adjacent roads. The square is the activity center (and has the tourist information center), so this should be your first port of call. From here it's just a brief walk to the Willamette River and Waterfront Park, where you can take a cruise or a stroll along the riverbank. I found keeping to the river's edge difficult as a number of adjacent attractions (Saturday market, sculptures, pocket gardens, street performers) tempt the walker away. The Pearl District, which has been beautifully regenerated in the last twenty years, is a reclaimed area of warehouses, now home to galleries, breweries, independent clothes stores, restaurants, coffee shops, and most importantly Powell's City of Books, housing over one million new and used books. You can spend an entire day here, and for anyone with an interest in books it is lethal. Visit at the end of the day when you think you have no energy left and watch how quickly three hours fly by. If in need of refreshment, visit the coffee bar in the store. Finally, no trip would be complete without a trip to Washington Park (a climb, but worth it and totally safe) to see the International Rose Test Garden and the tranquil Japanese Garden.

⟶ ADDITIONAL INFORMATION

The city does provide contrasts: a walk along a garbage-free, tree-lined neighborhood reveals independently owned, high-end retail stores, brightly painted, well-kept designer residences, artisanal gelatos for over $8 . . . and a number of homeless people sleeping on the streets. When taking an afternoon walk along the Willamette River bank, you may notice numerous panhandlers; my impression was that many of them had significant social and mental health issues. While I'm sympathetic to people who are less fortunate, I must admit I found their juxtaposition to families, tourists, and locals a bit unsettling.

Because Portland is a relatively small, beautiful city, the contrast between affluence and poverty there is more noticeable than in other cities.

As always, the independent woman needs to aware of the weather. Be prepared for rain no matter what month you visit. Portland has great cycle routes and is easy to explore by bike. It's the place for food, books, and independent craft breweries, for which it is becoming increasingly recognized; it also offers an array of cultural activities in the form of theaters, galleries, live performances, and festivals. Each weekend during the summer the city hosts an event in the main square.

In summary, the single woman will find Portland has great places to stay, is compact and easy to explore, has fantastic food, attractions, and shopping, and can be enjoyed at any time of the year. As long as the weather cooperates, a perfect sojourn awaits.

———➤ **WEBSITES**

portlandoregon.com
traveloregon.com
travelportland.com

SAVANNAH

Take Flight for

HISTORICAL SQUARES
SIZE
CULTURE

Savannah is amazing with the town squares and the hanging moss and the French Colonial houses. It's brutally romantic.

—David Morrissey

⟶ **IF UNSURE ABOUT TAKING A** trip to Savannah, read *Midnight in the Garden of Good and Evil* by John Berendt, watch the film, then commit. This old town (almost 300 years old!) oozes southern charm, and your time will be spent stumbling on the landmarks Berendt describes in his 1999 novel. At every street corner you'll see visitors reading it, and the coffee shops and restaurants he mentions are the most popular in town. The book has undoubtedly increased the draw of historical Savannah, but the real attractions are the buildings. Set among twenty-four unique squares and organized in a grid, beautifully restored houses, churches, and stores dating from the eighteenth and nineteenth centuries surround lush green lawns. Numerous oak and magnolia trees add a delightful aromatic aspect to wanderings. Savannah is a beautiful place for the single woman to explore, but it's not for those who want solitude. The best time to visit is at dawn (I kid you not) as from 9 AM to 4 PM the tour buses arrive and release a deluge of tourists who descend en masse to photograph and appreciate these squares. Savannah is anything but a well-kept secret. Apparently over fifty tour companies operate here, so if you decide not to go your own way, a wide variety of tour groups will offer to show you the sights. As I've said before, I'm not a tour group kind of gal, and during my three days in Savannah found more than enough to keep me entertained while walking and exploring the streets. Happily, avoiding the tour groups was not too much of an issue.

⟶ ARRIVAL

The Savannah/Hilton Head International Airport is relatively new, and from here taxi rates to the historical center are set at $25. The city is also served by Amtrak, but the rail station is a few miles west of the center of town.

⟶ ACCOMMODATIONS

Because Savannah is a highly popular yet relatively small tourist destination, accommodations there can be costly and difficult to find, although recently a number of newer hotels have opened. My understanding is that these have been able to keep up with demand. Securing a decent bed for the night for under $200 is difficult in the sought-after historical district. If you're a person who craves authenticity, style, and ambiance, consider a smaller hotel or a bed and breakfast and read the Trip Advisor comments before booking. Better bargains can be had out of town near the airport or in the Midtown, Southside, and West Chatham areas. I stayed for a conference in the large Hyatt hotel, which I initially thought of as alienating, but then was allocated a room overlooking the Savannah River where the views of the huge container ships provided unanticipated entertainment. I'd never been so close to these vessels, and after four days I grew to love the vista. I spent mornings opening my hotel bedroom curtains and waving to the sailors charged with delivering the huge containers fastened to their colossal ships. The Hyatt caused quite a stir when it was built in the 1980s, as its contemporary design was a stark contrast to the cobbled streets it straddles; in my opinion, it does look out of place. Book accommodations early and be aware that temperatures climb in the summer.

⟶ ACTIVITIES

Upon arrival, look out for the Visitors Information Center (301 Martin Luther King Boulevard), which is in a restored railway station, and collect the walking tour map; then set off to explore the twenty-four squares. This is a fantastic self-guided way to become acquainted and will take the better part of two days. The squares are unique and vary considerably in size. Be sure to take note of the other areas, such as markets, shops, and museums. Cobbled River Street—a must-see—is the tacky touristy center complete with souvenir shops, ice cream vendors, restaurants, and good views of the cargo ships. If an evening stroll is on the agenda, this is where the action is at night, and the area is quite safe, as many other people walk here. One of the most popular sights is the Mercer-William House Museum, which plays a significant role in the famous book mentioned above. I also recommend a trip to the **Ralph Mark Gilbert Civil Rights Museum**, where the tour groups are few and far between, and, of course, to the birthplace of the founder of the Girl Scouts, Juliette Gordon Low.

⟶ ADDITIONAL INFORMATION

"Life is like a box of chocolates—you never know what you're going to get!" said Tom Hanks in the 1994 film *Forrest Gump*, some of which was filmed in Savannah. The secret is to pick out the chocolates you think you will like. Savannah is a unique, historical southern-belle town featuring twenty-four squares and parks, ideal for slow walks and exploration; like boxed chocolates, each square is different—you never know which one you'll discover next. Avoid visiting in July and August when the temperatures can be scorching, or during St. Patrick's Day when the population doubles. Come with a good amount of money; accommodations are expensive. Savannah is a destination for the cultured girl, and should the need for company take over, look for a trolley bus tour, a ghost tour, a walking tour, a food tour, a movie tour, a little-known Savannah tour, a bike tour, or an eco-tour; each year the offerings grow. I found Savannah to be a very safe city; as it is compact and visitors are numerous, walking and exploring during the day and early evenings present no issues.

—→ **WEBSITES**

exploregeorgia.org

savannah.com

savannahvisit.com

visitsavannah.com

SANTA FE

Take Flight for

ART
GALLERIES
SHOPPING

This was the place for me. I felt immediately at home; I have never felt so quickly, so comfortably, so immediately attracted.

—Richard Bradford

⟶ **THE OFFICIAL 2015 SANTA FE** Guide states that the city has been voted one of the top ten cities in the world. When I mentioned to girlfriends I was writing a book on women's travel, many of them remarked that the book would not be complete without including Santa Fe. So I made a special trip in May 2015 to see what all the fuss was about. If you love art, jewelry, museums, galleries, spas, and shopping, Santa Fe and its little sister Taos are the places to be. Galleries and independently owned stores full of one-of-a-kind merchandise bustle with shoppers. The city is small and compact, so walking to access all the attractions is not an issue. Fitness and even those comfortable shoes I constantly harp on about are not as vital as in other cities. Restrooms are plentiful and easily located. It is so totally a gal place. I could not get over how many women over the age of forty were wandering the streets, shopping bags in hand, clad in loose-fitting designer shirts and bright harem pants. Women of every size and shape were chattering and laughing in packs or even by themselves. Men were few and far between, and the men I saw seemed embarrassed to be there.

Within a two-mile square are over 250 galleries (after New York and Los Angeles, Santa Fe has the next highest concentration of galleries and artists in the USA), over 250 restaurants, fourteen museums, and hundreds of jewelry, clothing, and antique stores; there is even a glossy brochure listing the consignment boutiques. Shopping paradise or what!

At over four hundred years old, Santa Fe is the oldest capital in the USA, has over three hundred days a year of sunshine, and at an elevation of over seven thousand feet is also the highest capital in the country. The biggest disadvantage in planning a trip is that it is not easy to access, and for most visitors two flights are required. Also, if art and shopping are not high priorities, then other US cities may be more appealing. Having said that, the city offers a wealth of activities and excursions to experience, and road trips on the barren New Mexican terrain are gorgeous. Of all the cities listed in this book, Santa Fe is one of the safest I've visited and is by far the most female oriented, and although I'm not a shopper, I can easily understand the gal appeal.

→ ARRIVAL

Santa Fe is not easy to get to. Although flying from a number of US cities (e.g., Dallas, Chicago, New York) to Albuquerque is possible, from here the options are to rent a car and drive for one hour to Santa Fe, or to take the shuttle bus or train. Direct flights are available to Santa Fe from Dallas, Denver, and Los Angeles, but unless you live within easy access of these hubs, getting here will take time. Amtrak has a service to Lamy, eighteen miles away, and there is a Greyhound service. Visiting the community without your own transportation is possible, but, I know I wouldn't have enjoyed my five-night stay to the extent I did if I hadn't had access to a vehicle. And if you want to see more—especially if you want to visit Taos, which I do recommend—then a car is essential.

→ ACCOMMODATIONS

The best-located hotels are the most expensive within the old historical downtown core. La Fonda is a wonderful family-run hotel and tourist attraction that should be on every visitor's agenda, even if for most of us it's way too expensive. The ornate, heavily tiled restrooms are well worth a visit, as is the court-yard restaurant and upper galleries' art. Other really expensive accommodations offer spa treatments and girlfriend packages. Santa Fe does have a range of more reasonably priced accommodations away from the historic downtown (therefore requiring transportation); many of these establishments are located on Cerrillos Road, which has little to credit it in terms of historic charm or attractions. Rates can be reasonable in the low season of January and February but peak during the summer and during the famous Indian Christmas Market, when accommodations should be booked six months in advance. Many non-chain establishments promote their New Mexican ethnic decorations and ambiance.

⟶ ACTIVITIES

Unless one is a serious shopper and/or art buff, two full days in this historical city are quite adequate to empty the wallet and visit the galleries, museums, and shops. Santa Fe can be divided into three areas: downtown, the Railyard District, and Canyon Road. A visit downtown must include the Georgia O'Keefe museum and the New Mexican Museum of Art. If planning to see more museums, including those in Taos, consider purchasing a museum pass. The downtown core is not large and has the highest concentration of shops, many located in multilevel arcades, which inspire more exploration. The main plaza is in the center of town and is a great place to consume ice cream on a park bench and organize purchases. The Railyard is a concentration of art galleries and retail establishments, formerly warehouses, and is a brief walk from central Santa Fe. When I visited this district it was quite deserted but provided a nice contrast to downtown. I questioned the tourism information gal about the lack of people, and she told me that Santa Fe is always quiet, except between June and September; Friday nights during the summer are apparently the best time to visit. Canyon Road is *the* place for art; over eighty galleries line the street. Here not just wall art, but also huge sculptures are on offer. If art is your passion, you can spend an entire day here as everyone who operates a gallery is enthusiastic to talk to anyone who enters it. While I usually like speaking to locals, after entry to only three galleries I decided time in Santa Fe was too precious to be learning about every artist's life history, so I observed their art from a safe distance. From Santa Fe you can take a number of highly rewarding trips. For example, for the amazingly economical fare of $10 return (2015 price), enjoy the ninety-minute train trip to Albuquerque across the barren New Mexico landscape. This fare includes free bus rides in the city. Visitors with their own transport should make the circle tour to Taos, a smaller version of Santa Fe. In many respects I preferred this town; it had fewer tourists and seemed less commercial, but still had a pretty square and numerous shops and galleries. From Taos it is a brief twenty-minute drive to the famous Rio Grande River and the bridge, which offers photographic opportunities. Finally, try to visit Los Alamos, famous for the exploration of nuclear technology. In a couple of hours, you can visit two very informative (free) museums that provide a fascinating history with interesting films for those of us who are not science enthusiasts—it's a welcome alternative to all that art and shopping.

> ADDITIONAL INFORMATION

Santa Fe is a compact city that offers the shopping/art queen a Mecca of attractions, but to get the most out of it, you need to rent a vehicle. After three days (or maybe just two if shopping is not on the agenda), it's time to travel farther afield to Albuquerque, Los Alamos, and especially Taos. What I enjoyed the most was driving on the barren roads across the New Mexico landscape, which brought to mind Butch Cassidy and the Sundance Kid. The geography is very distinctive and for this traveler a wonderful surprise. Seeing the Rio Grande cut through the stark landscape was unforgettable. Unless you're accustomed to very hot temperatures, avoid the baking heat and crowds of July and August; shoulder seasons are ideal times to visit. Finally, if you're seeking a holiday that provides familiarity with fellow travelers, Santa Fe delivers. Unlike all other cities included in this book (which appeal to every age and both sexes), I cannot imagine many young women on limited budgets (or men of any age, for that matter) having Santa Fe high on their list of places to see, unless they have a strong interest in art.

All told, it is the most accommodating city for the single female traveler *and* for those who seek a girlfriend getaway; having company will make shopping more sociable—if you want company, that is—and Santa Fe is such a delightful, artsy place to boot.

⟶ **WEBSITES**

newmexico.org
santafe.org
santafenm.gov

VANCOUVER

Take Flight for

NATURAL BEAUTY
SAFETY
STANLEY PARK

I love just how beautiful Vancouver is: I mean, everywhere
you look it's just mountains and ocean.

—Emma Bell

⟶ **IN 1984, WHILE LIVING IN** Ottawa, I traveled to Vancouver
for the first time for a brief five-day holiday. Its oceanfront location surrounded by snow-capped mountains was breathtaking.
The people were friendly, and each told the same apocryphal
story about being able to ski in the mountains in the morning
and swim in the ocean during the afternoon. It was as if each
Vancouverite had sworn a pact to smile and enthusiastically tell
the same anecdote to every tourist they encountered.

Vancouver is now my home and has been for the last
twenty-five years, so I may not be objective enough to write

about it as a tourist. Since my arrival I've seen the population double and the house prices quadruple. A house cannot be purchased in Vancouver for anything less than $1 million; in fact, the city has the second-highest housing costs in the world, just after Hong Kong. Even so, I am still in love with the place to the extent that, despite hundreds of return trips home, I cannot read when flying on a clear day; instead I press my face up against the window of the aircraft in awe of the mountains, valleys, lakes, and fjords the plane flies over during its approach to Vancouver. For the single woman, Vancouver is a breeze to explore; it's safe, affluent, new, and easy. September is the best month, as there are fewer visitors and the weather is generally good. But be sure to bring an umbrella—it can rain a lot.

⟶ **ARRIVAL**

I am, of course, totally biased, but YVR—Vancouver International Airport—is one of the best airports in the world. (Ironically, I'm writing the first draft of this book while seated in Houston International Airport, where it is impossible to find a non-food-court area to sit and write; Starbucks doesn't even have its own tables!) YVR has a floor-to-ceiling ocean fish tank in the international departure lounge, numerous sofas and comfortable seats, First Nations art and sculptures, designer shops, restaurants, and reasonably priced food outlets. The departure area found prior to check-in houses the most amazing, huge Bill Reid bronze sculpture. Taxis from the airport to downtown are under $45 and sometimes limousines offering similar prices are available. Alternatively, the SkyTrain offers a convenient, economical ($8) thirty-minute journey to central Vancouver and operates until the early hours of the morning. Both options are safe. Buses and trains (Amtrak and VIA Rail) arrive at the Central Station, which is well connected by the SkyTrain to the city, a brief five-minute trip. It's not a great location to spend time, but compared to other North American cities it's quite safe.

⟶ ACCOMMODATIONS

Vancouver has a good (if heavily used) transit system, so if accommodations in the downtown core are too pricey or unavailable (demand can be high during the summer months and during special events), then consider hotels near the airport. From here taking the SkyTrain to central Vancouver takes about thirty minutes. Because there is an abundance of coffee bars and restaurants, choosing a hotel with breakfast services should not be a priority. The best-located hotels are the ones near Stanley Park or on the waterfront, but these can be expensive. Most hotels have been constructed in the last thirty years, so they offer new spacious facilities; there are also a growing number of designer boutique hotels should you have the means and desire to splurge.

⟶ ACTIVITIES

Where to start? Vancouver is not the city to choose if you crave culture, architecture, history, the latest fashion, or galleries and museums (although the Museum of Anthropology at University of British Columbia is well worth a visit). The city is very young and has few buildings over one hundred years old. Vancouver is the location of the best park in the world—Stanley Park. Everyone who visits should take the fourteen-kilometer stroll around the seawall, which follows the water around the perimeter and from where it is possible to spot seals, bald eagles, otters, and other wildlife. Alternatively, rent a bike to complete the same route. The park has a gorgeous aquarium, as well as a great outdoor swimming pool. Plan to spend a day in Stanley Park no matter what the season.

The reclaimed industrial area of Granville Island has a huge variety of artisans and craft shops, theaters, restaurants, a food market, and street performers, and is a lovely rabbit warren to explore. From here you can take little water taxis to other destinations, such as Stanley Park and Science World. One of the most famous tourist sites is the Capilano Suspension Bridge; a free bus operates from downtown to this attraction. Or you can try the free alternative at Lynn Canyon, which is far less touristy and provides access to a number of walking trails into the rainforest mountains. If the weather is good, check out Kitsilano Pool (which used to be the largest outdoor swimming pool in the Commonwealth) or the beaches of Spanish Banks. The downtown core has shopping centered around Robson Street. Finally, if you visit during the summer months, consider a night of open air theater at Bard on the Beach (www.bardonthebeach .com). Even if you're not a Shakespeare fan, the outside ambiance, quality of performance, and reasonably priced tickets will convert you.

⟶ ADDITIONAL INFORMATION

Now for the downside: there are two main blots on the face of this city (even though the international media consistently name it one of the best places in the world to live): the weather and the Downtown Eastside area. Vancouver is in a rainforest, so it can rain, and rain, and rain. Some visitors spend a week in the city and never see the mountains (which are visible on clear days from the downtown core) due to the moist gloom. This can be a particular problem if you visit anytime from October to April, but can occur during any month of the year. The Downtown Eastside is an area of acute poverty with a high concentration of individuals who suffer from drug addiction or mental illness. The area is adjacent to the tourist regions of Chinatown and Gastown. While it embarrasses me that in such an affluent country and in such a rich city these social issues are not being adequately addressed, the area is relatively safe compared to many of the other North American cities featured in this book. While these two issues need to be considered, they should not prevent any woman from visiting what the British *Daily Telegraph* newspaper described as the second-best city to visit in 2014 (after Cape Town).

—→ WEBSITES

hellobc.com

tourismvancouver.com

vancouverattractions.com

vancouvertourist.com

WHISTLER

Take Flight for

← →

**OUTDOORS
SMALL COMMUNITY
MOUNTAINS**

I would say a must-do in Canada would be to go skiing at
Whistler . . . you take a car lift for, like, a half hour to the
top of this mountain, and you ski down and it takes, like,
so long to get to the bottom. You go past the clouds. It's
absolutely incredible.

—Sebastian Bach

——→ **I HAVE SELECTED WHISTLER AS** a destination primarily for
the woman who wants to do something physical during a single
sojourn, and get a great deal when doing so. This relatively small
ski town is located a couple of hours north of Vancouver, British
Columbia; Vancouver International (YVR) is the nearest airport.
Whistler was originally developed as a ski resort but is now a
year-round destination, and is especially attractive to people
who like the outdoors. I am not a skier and do not like the cold,
so I visit Whistler in the off-season, which is between April and
November; this is when prices for accommodations are very,

very reasonable, the vast crowds are gone, the temperatures are warm, and the scenery is spectacular. It is not the destination for the ardent shopper, the culture freak, or the designer gal. The town itself can be easily explored in a day, and if communing with nature is not on your to-do list, visit Vancouver instead. But if you have a passion for cycling, white water rafting, hiking, skiing, exercising, swimming, or just taking a leisurely stroll in breathtaking scenery, then indulge in those activities; reward yourself with an end-of-day trip to the hot tub, read those novels that have been on your bedside table for ages, and give yourself some much-needed pampering time.

⟶ ARRIVAL

In 1985 I drove from Vancouver to Whistler on the Sea-to-Sky Highway, which skirts the mountains and looks over spectacular fjords. I thought it to be the most beautiful road in the world. In 1991 I moved to British Columbia and again traveled this route. Now, many experiences—like reunions with old boyfriends—fail to live up to our previous fond memories, but the 134-kilometer (eighty-three mile) Sea-to-Sky Highway delivered again. I still maintain it to be one of the most spectacular roads on the planet (I know the Great Ocean Road in Australia is supposed to be, but having experienced both I think the Sea-to-Sky one is way better). You can travel from the Vancouver airport to Whistler by rental car, bus (approximately $70 one way), or by private shuttle service. Buses also depart from downtown Vancouver. While I recommend hiring a car, a perfectly fun time can be had using public transport, which is safe and economical—and as most accommodations in Whistler demand a fee for parking, taking public transit can work out to be much cheaper than renting a car.

→ ACCOMMODATIONS

Prices for accommodations in Whistler fluctuate tremendously depending on the season. The Fairmont Hotel offers rooms for as little as $200 per night in the low season, then advertise the same room for over $1,000 during the Christmas holidays. In addition to a number of hotels, various lodges offer self-catering accommodations, from studios to three-bedroom suites (www.resortquestwhistler.com). These are fully equipped with kitchens; most have exercise rooms, pools, hot tubs, lounge areas, and parking, and are only a short distance from the ski hills—ideal for the woman who wants to cater to herself. Be aware that car parking fees can be considerable at these locations. Some of the lodges are above retail outlets in town and may be a little noisier than others located farther away in the adjacent Blackcomb area. In my experience, a girl can get a lot of bang for her buck when staying outside of the main ski season. If you opt to stay in one of the numerous lodges, away from the central core area, taking pleasant walks to and from accommodations along the well-cared-for trails is a delightful way to relax and appreciate the quiet, spectacular location.

→ ACTIVITIES

From the first week of December until the last week of April, the primary activity is skiing. This is when prices for accommodations are highest; after this, costs decline. In subsequent months, mountain biking, cycling (there are over 40 kilometers of wonderful paved, easy, flat cycle paths), hiking on clearly marked trails or on cross-country ski routes, canoeing, paddle boarding, golf, white water rafting, swimming (at a hotel pool or in Lost Lake) are on offer. Bikes of every shape and size are available for rent. The gondola to the top of Whistler Mountain operates year-round, and from there the Peak 2 Peak Gondola provides superb views and leads to easy alpine walking trails. Bears are frequently spotted in the vicinity, but this should not discourage anyone from exploring. For the adventurous, there is zip lining; for the less adventurous, spas and massage treatments. And if it rains, the large leisure center has hot tubs, pool, a gym, and exercise classes. Whistler has something for everyone.

———> **ADDITIONAL INFORMATION**

Most of the destinations recommended in this text have been included for their architectural significance (well, perhaps not Vegas!) and have sizable populations, but Whistler's allure is in its natural beauty; it's a small, purpose-built ski resort with clean air, glacier-fed, aqua-blue streams and rivers, clear lakes, and huge snowcapped mountains. It delivers an "away-from-it-all" experience while still providing the luxuries of coffee shops, a car-free pedestrian township, and a safe environment. There are no panhandlers, dilapidated buildings, graffiti, abandoned houses, or litter, and everyone is either on holiday or employed in the tourism industry. You'll hear more Australian and British accents here than you will North American ones as Whistler recruits a number of students from across the globe to work in this tourist mecca. While no people threaten visitors, black bears are frequently encountered on the trails around Whistler. They can easily be avoided by backing away, and while a certain level of vigilance is required, they are not a problem for tourists. Walking around town is the norm, and in the summer there are a number of festivals and open-air concerts. While a certain income is required to ski here, once that cohort has left town Whistler opens its doors to the outdoorsy woman and offers her a multitude of physical and spiritual experiences to stretch the mind and body. After a few days, fellow travelers recognize each other, the guys working in the grocery store greet you as an old friend, roads and trails become familiar, and Whistler feels like home. It's the perfect location if your energy needs to be recharged through clean air and nature. For the lady who likes the outdoors and her own company, there is no better, safer place.

⟶ **WEBSITES**

hello-bc.com

whistler.com

whistlerblackcomb.com

whistlerchamber.com

TIME TO TAKE FLIGHT
IN EUROPE

LONDON

Take Flight for

CROWDS
MUSEUMS
THEATER

When a man is tired of London, he is tired of life; for there
is in London all that life can afford.

—Samuel Johnson

⟶ **FOR A CONSIDERABLE NUMBER OF** North Americans, London
is *the* city in Europe to visit. Many have ambitions to see it in
three days. Others believe seven days will be needed, and some
consider two weeks to be ample. All these time frames are
inadequate for even a basic understanding of this metropolis
of 8.6 million people. London is huge and, compared with
other European cities such as Paris or Amsterdam, spread
out. The sanitized, perfect images we have all seen soon melt
away when the logistics of moving from point A to point B
in this city are realized. I lived in London for over two years

and have visited on countless occasions. I love it on cold rainy days from November to February. Almost seventeen million tourists visit London each year and fewer are there during these winter months. When making decisions about a trip to London, you must accept that seeing it all is impossible; it will be very expensive, it will be impossible to feel alone, and quiet time is not going to happen, but upon leaving you'll want to return to see more. Every day is an adventure offering new, unexpected things to stimulate all of the senses. There are just so many possibilities within the city, from where to stay, to what to do, to how much to spend. And despite being huge, this metropolis welcomes the female traveler who has the energy and enthusiasm to discover everything seen on BBC and more. Start planning and saving now.

⟶ ARRIVAL

Although somewhat dirty and old in comparison to many transportation systems in Europe and North America, the public transport system in London is a generally good, but heavily used. Arrival by air from North America will be at either Heathrow (one of the busiest airports in the world, but with good shopping upon departure) or Gatwick Airport. From Heathrow, the options are the (slow) underground/ subway system, taking about an hour, which is cheap but not recommended for the single, tired, jet-lagged, luggage-dragging woman unless accommodations are close to the Piccadilly or District Line tube stops. Alternatively there is a fast train, the Heathrow Express, which takes only fifteen minutes. This is on the most expensive section of rail track in the UK but is very convenient (about $45 one way). The train arrives at

Paddington Station, from which taxis or the underground will take you to your destination. A taxi from Heathrow Airport to central London will cost about €50 (US $70) and will take about an hour (depending on traffic and where you want to go). Gatwick Airport is located south of London, and from here the Gatwick Express Train takes passengers on the thirty-minute trip to Victoria Station. Be warned: this—and many other trains in England—can be very crowded. National Express operates a bus service from both airports to Victoria Coach Station in central London and is a good alternative if plans include travel to other English towns.

ACCOMMODATIONS

Expensive—this is the word best used to describe accommodations in London. While the options are extensive, many people find the prices, even for a moderate hotel, excessive. Expect small rooms, dubious plumbing, and old, tired furnishings in many mid-range three-star hotels. Some of the cheaper rooms do not have en suite bathrooms. But it is not all bad news: London is so expansive that taking the Tube will be part of every visitor's experience. Securing a centrally located hotel in the desirable West End, while lovely if you can afford it, is not necessary; inevitably, you will use the public transit system. Locations that have a good offering of moderately priced hotels include Earls Court, Victoria, Kensington, Pimlico, and Notting Hill. Many include the iconic fried British breakfast, but if they do not, alternatives exist on every street corner. There is also an abundance of bed and breakfast options (but be warned, some of these may be more expensive than larger hotel chains). Decide on where you want to be and then select a hotel in

this area. Consider UK chain hotels like Premier Inn (www
.premiertravelinn.co.uk), ibis (www.ibis.com), and Travelodge
(www.travelodge.co.uk). No areas are particularly dangerous
to the single woman, but keep in mind that if you select more
reasonably priced accommodations in the suburbs, you'll spend
considerable time traveling.

──> ACTIVITIES

The Tower of London, St. Paul's, Tower Bridge, Buckingham
Palace, the London Eye, the Globe Theater, Westminster Abbey,
the Houses of Parliament, Nelson's Column, Covent Garden,
Camden Bridge—the list goes on and on before the stage is
even set for the famous museums and galleries (Victoria and
Albert, Natural History, Tate). And then there is the shopping
(Harrods, Selfridges, Marks and Spencer), the parks (Hyde,
Green, Regent's) the theaters, the restaurants, and the pubs.
Decide on priorities and make a plan. Take a "hop on hop off"
bus tour or take an actual tour (often the thing to do on a first
day to get over the jet lag and familiarize yourself with the city's
layout), or the Thames River trip down to Greenwich.

London is exhausting. Many of the attractions get incredibly
busy during the summer months, and just coping with the sheer
number of people who walk along Oxford Street, cross at the
crowded intersections, or descend on the escalators to take the
subway trains is shocking to those who don't usually encounter
such an intense volume of human beings. Navigating this throng
also takes time. As mentioned earlier, my favorite months to
visit London are between November and February (but not at
Christmas). Many of the attractions can be seen in the wet and
cold (it rarely snows) as long as you're prepared. Museums are

better seen first thing in the day when your legs and eyes are fresh, your energy level is high, and visitors are fewer. For the most popular attractions (Madame Tussauds, Tower of London, London Eye, Westminster Abbey) consider booking in advance. Save shopping on Oxford Street and Regent Street, and in Knightsbridge and Kensington until the end of the day, and feel your weariness give way to liveliness as each department store entices. Finally, find respite from the highest concentration of crowds by venturing beyond the city center; you can easily take public transit to places such as Kew Gardens and Windsor Castle—and remember to try the cruise to Greenwich down the Thames.

⟶ ADDITIONAL INFORMATION

London is big, busy, and noisy. It may appear dirty and edgy, but it has a unique culture. While the city is home to newcomers from every corner of the world, so many things here are quaint and quintessentially British, from the "bobbies" (police officers) to the public telephone boxes, to black taxis, fish and chip cafés, and pubs. London is safe for the single mature woman day and night. Still, it's always wise to exercise street smarts in tourist destinations. Going to see a West End show that finishes at 11 PM and then taking the subway ("Tube") back to your hotel is not at all threatening, as so many other women will be doing exactly the same. Yes, there is petty crime and opportunistic theft, but London is far safer than most North American cities. London has the most expensive public transport system in the world, so you would be wise to invest in a multi-day transit pass—the Visitor Oyster Travelcard—for ease and convenience. In the UK the British pound is still used, although most service industries accept the euro (€). And although everyone (of course) speaks English, the accents can be difficult to understand and take a bit of getting used to. Now, back to my favorite subject: while the quality, age, and overall cleanliness of restrooms in certain locations leave something to be desired, they are generally available, frequently require a fee on entry, normally demand waiting in line, and are often devoid of toilet tissue, so make sure you carry supplies; your stash of tissues and hand sanitizer will certainly come in handy. A few months ago, I arrived at the very busy St. Pancras International Train Station in London with my suitcase. Good news: the restrooms were open and no payment was required; bad news: I needed to wait ten minutes in a line adjacent to the men's facilities (where there was of course no queue). When I did finally arrive at the cubicle, I couldn't get in with my suitcase. I sat in my cramped, prized cubicle listening to the station announcement tell me not to leave luggage unattended while my belongings languished unattended outside the stall for other women to trip over. While there are so many wonderful things in this iconic city to adore, there are many that frustrate, fascinate, and entertain this North American visitor.

---→ **WEBSITES**

londontourism.com
visitbritain.com
visitlondon.com

PARIS

Take Flight for

WALKING
SHOPPING
CHIC

Paris is always a good idea.

—Audrey Hepburn

⟶ AH, PARIS—WHAT IS THERE NOT to like? Okay, maybe the waiters in the traditional Parisian cafés could do with a bit of customer service training, but other than that, Paris is a compact, architecturally wonderful city, and a delight for the solo girl to explore. Smaller and more navigable than other European cities such as London, Berlin, or Rome, Paris is a walkable international city with oodles of style and class, and is the self-proclaimed intellectual center for art, fashion, and literature. Easy to get lost in, packed with traffic, designer chic women (and men), and the most beautiful buildings, Paris seems to have ignored all the twenty-first-century environmental pressure to take the cars off the street. While Paris is an incredibly noisy, bustling center, you can easily leave the congestion behind and wander among quaint back streets to explore real Parisian life. Here is a more down-to-earth human side, with small boulangeries and cafés and a vibrant, entertaining street scene.

At the age of twenty-one, I had my first three-course *plat du jour* alone in a restaurant in Paris, and whenever I return, I pass by this establishment in the Latin Quarter to do the same. I have stayed here on at least ten occasions in cheap, run-down, disastrous hotels as well as designer four-star abodes. I have visited the City of Lights in the height of summer and the depth of winter and never get bored. If a city can immediately alter one's well-being, that city is Paris. It's like breathing different air upon entry and discovering a new you. Yes, I know many complain over the lack of free refills of coffee, ice-free drinks, toilets that are not the cleanest in the world, showers offering weak dribbles of lukewarm water, and the aloof Parisian manner, but despite all these limitations there is a undeniable *je ne sais quoi*. Although you need to use your street smarts, for the most part the city is not at all a threatening place, even at night. This, along with its compact size and romantic reputation, makes Paris inviting for the single girl.

⟶ ARRIVAL

Paris is easy to get to from North America as there are many direct flights. Two airports serve Paris: Charles de Gaulle, twenty-three kilometers northeast of the city, and Orly, fourteen kilometers south. RER (Réseau Express Régional) commuter trains operate from Charles de Gaulle and offer the most economical (though time-consuming) way to reach the city center. This mode of transportation also involves walking some distance with luggage. I prefer the airport vans, which should be booked in advance but are reliable and provide door-to-door service (about €30) no matter the time of arrival. Taxis can be expensive at €70 or more, depending on time of day and traffic. Orly is a small airport, so to access the metro from the airport a shuttle is provided to the RER-B line. Door-to-door van shuttles are around €30, taxis about €60.

——> ACCOMMODATIONS

The single North American woman must do some serious research when deciding on Parisian accommodations. I thought my single dorm bed during university undergraduate days was narrow until I stayed in a three-and-a-half-star Best Western hotel in Paris. I could not swing a mouse, let alone a cat. If you have considerable funds, fantastic large rooms are available. The rest of us have to lower our cultural expectations and accept accommodations that are smaller and sometimes without elevators, air conditioning, or tea/coffee-making facilities. The last time I stayed in Paris, I requested a room that *didn't* face the street because I wanted to avoid the noise. I was given a small, hot, fifth-floor (no elevator) attic room that overlooked a courtyard. It would have been perfect except for the croissants baked at 4 AM in the adjacent bakery, from which an overpowering smell came through the skylight, permeating my room. I gained four pounds just from the aroma. Unlike the star rating for many other European cities, the star rating for Parisian hotels is difficult to fathom. Breakfast, when it is included, tends to be coffee and croissants, so eating out is preferable. Reserve ahead for the best rates, and narrow the extensive choice of hotels by choosing an area in which you want to stay. I like the Latin Quarter (Left Bank) or, a little farther out in Montmartre, Pigalle, and the twenty arrondissements (government defined areas), which have a range of boutique hotels in a charming but hilly area. Avoid hotels around Gare du Nord, though, as the area is not particularly safe or welcoming after dark.

→ ATTRACTIONS

Paris is a city divided into twenty arrondissements within a ring road. At barely twelve kilometers in length it's a compact city centered around the Seine River; I have always found Paris very easy to navigate and explore. If you go there, keep in mind its popularity. In 2014 it was the most popular tourist destination in the world and received over thirty-two million visitors, so if you plan to see the most famous attractions (Louvre, Eiffel Tower, Rodin Museum, Musée d'Orsay, Versailles, etc.), purchase tickets online to avoid the queues; failure to do so means precious tourism hours wasted in line. Wander along the banks of the Seine—or even take a boat trip—to get a feel for the geography of the city, and try the evening riverboat trip if visiting in spring or summer. Visit the Grand Magasins, especially Galleries Lafayette, and make an effort to visit Basilique Sacré Cœur—the adjacent neighborhood is a lovely introduction to Parisian back lanes, and the view of the surrounding city from this white edifice is spectacular. Make time to visit an array of the numerous cafés, and watch the price of a café au lait (coffee with milk) rise and fall.

───➤ **ADDITIONAL INFORMATION**

You can explore Paris at any time of the year if you wear appropriate attire, but the weather can become quite hot in July and August. August is the month Parisians leave town for cooler climates, but it is not quieter then, as the tourists still come in droves. In such a tourist mecca there is really no quiet time. Restrooms are somewhat few and far between, and a few cafés still have the hole-in-the-floor option (also known as a "squat" or "Turkish" toilet), so be prepared. Fast-food restaurants print the toilet access code on receipts—worth the price of a coffee or bottle of water. As mentioned earlier, the area around Gare du Nord is not a welcoming place at night; crimes of opportunity are common, especially theft from backpacks around tourist destinations such as the Eiffel Tower, Sacré Cœur, and Pompidou Center, and on the metro. Scams are also a way to dupe tourists. Again, take sensible precautions. France uses the euro (€) and tipping is not always expected. Everyone in the service industry speaks English, but, being French, they may not want to. Be especially careful when crossing roads, as traffic seems to come from every direction and can be in the form of a van, car, moped, bike, or all four. Try to tag along with others when crossing intersections. Finally, be prepared to feel a bit dowdy and plain; Parisian women live up to their international reputation for being chic, adding to the glamorous appeal that is quintessentially Paris.

───➤ **WEBSITES**

girlsguidetoparis.com
goparis.about.com
parisinfo.com
paristouristoffice.com

ROME

Take Flight for

ANCIENT CULTURE
CHURCHES
ART

Rome is the city of echoes, the city of illusions, and the city of yearning.

—Giotto di Bondone

⟶ **IN PARIS, TRAFFIC IS THE** greatest source of noise; in Rome, it's the traffic *and* the people. A bustling city with a devil-may-care attitude, Rome—the first capital city in the world and home to the Catholic church—is the center of European civilization. The Romans know how to live loudly, drink well, and display an exceedingly robust confidence. In everything they do, they are aware that they live among the world's most breathtaking ancient buildings (along with Paris and London, Rome displays the best architecture in Europe). They take pride in a culture others feel privileged to visit, if only for a brief time.

If you're a nervous gal planning your first-ever solo trip, Rome is perhaps not the best European city on which to cut your international traveling teeth; you may want to try Amsterdam, Vienna, or Edinburgh first. But if you're a plucky dame who can handle a noisy, intimidating city, and if you love museums, paintings, and buildings, then go for it.

Rome is a bit trickier for the single woman to visit than other European cities such as London, Amsterdam, or Paris, because it is less safe at night and suffers from petty crime; it's also larger and therefore more difficult to navigate. Add to this the chaotic traffic and aggressive drivers who do not seem to obey rules of the road. English, while widely used, is not universal, and the resident population is not as friendly and accommodating as in other European cities (unless you are a young attractive woman—then there is more than enough attention from a certain demographic). Also, tourists frequently end up paying more for commodities than anticipated. With all these negatives, why do I encourage you to visit? Because if you're well prepared, remain optimistic for the first twenty-four hours, and accept the city's limitations, the cultural wealth Rome offers makes up for any shortcomings. My first day alone in Rome was anything but stress free, but as each of my four days elapsed I gained more confidence, obtained an understanding of the geography, traffic, and men, and eventually relaxed by taking the "when in Rome" approach. Subsequent visits were easier as my acceptance and understanding of the culture improved, and I now have no hesitation in visiting.

⟶ **ARRIVAL**

If it's been forty-five minutes after your arrival at Leonardo da Vinci (Fiumicino) International Airport and your luggage has not yet emerged on the baggage conveyer belt, don't panic; this is normal. On three occasions in the last five years I have had this experience. Welcome to Rome! At least when your belongings are eventually retrieved (hopefully!) you can look forward to an easy train ride to the city center on the Leonardo Express (€14), which takes about thirty minutes and is safe, although traveling this route through graffiti-smeared, dilapidated buildings does not give an ideal first impression. There are also airport shuttles (€27) and taxis (€60 or more), but these can take over an hour, as the traffic is very chaotic and heavy. The other airport is Ciampino, fifteen kilometers southeast. From here the options to the city center are a shuttle bus at €25 or a taxi for around €30. All trains, both from within the country and outside, arrive at Stazione Termini, which is reputed to be not the safest of locations, so use your street smarts and make a quick exit. It is also huge, so be prepared to wheel that suitcase quite a distance along station platforms before exiting.

—> ACCOMMODATIONS

The key to finding accommodations is to book early, as Rome is very popular, especially if you're planning to visit between April and July or September and October. There is a range of accommodations, from expensive five-star hotels to small family-run lodgings. The most desirable locations are near tourist attractions (Colosseum, Roman Forum), as well as the Centro Storico, Tridente, Trevi, and Quirinale areas. A more economical option is the area around Stazione Termini; while not very welcoming at night, it's a good central alternative if, like me, you plan to be in your room by 7 PM. During one visit, I stayed in a large Sheraton away from the city center; it offered complimentary shuttle service from the airport to the hotel and free transportation four times a day to and from the Colosseum. This hotel was a great, quiet alternative and paid for itself because of the complimentary transportation. Air conditioning is not always available and is vital in July and August. Prices decrease in the quieter winter months.

—→ ACTIVITIES

Use a really, really good map to explore Rome—but even with this, expect to get lost. Wear good shoes; a lot of walking is required. Come with lots of energy so you can see as much as possible—there is a lot to see. As in most European cities in the twenty-first century, if you want to see the hot spots without lining up, you must book online in advance. Sometimes opting to take an organized tour and paying a little more can fast-track the entry process. This happened to me at the Colosseum: instead of waiting in line for two hours, for an additional €5 I joined an organized tour for immediate entry. It can become very, very hot in the summer months, so at these times consider taking a siesta and visiting sites in the evening hours. I visited the Vatican Square at 6:30 PM in June, and although I could not gain access, I was amazed at how few tourists were there, a complete contrast to a previous visit at midday when the tour buses had disgorged gazillions of visitors and when it was anything but a tranquil experience. Seeing the square when few people are there is far better, but if ensuring access is a priority, book in advance. Likewise, the Trevi Fountain is best seen at 9 AM; after this it is very crowded and that selfie will include at least ten other people. In addition to seeing the Colosseum, Pantheon, Vatican, and St. Peter's Basilica, wander into every church you see—you'll be amazed at the art, structure, and artifacts that have escaped the notice of Fodor's. Entry to these buildings is often a nice excuse to cool down and rest; carry a scarf, as some require head and arm coverings. Consider buying the Roma Pass, which provides free access to a range of galleries, museums, and archeological sites, as well as free transportation.

⟶ ADDITIONAL INFORMATION

The single female needs to be aware of a number of things when considering a visit to Rome. It is a big city; petty crime is an issue, particularly pick-pocketing and bag theft, which are more prevalent here than in other large European cities such as London and Paris. That said, it is still safer than many North American cities; again, street smarts are required. Drivers often decide to ignore red lights or signage, so when crossing the road, look for someone else to cross with and walk close to them—safety in numbers. Pairing up also helps diffuse aggression: when a driver shouts abuse he will have to direct it at both of you, which is slightly less unnerving. Even more dangerous than car drivers are scooter operators, as they seem to act under a law unto themselves. Toilets are not plentiful, but all cafés and restaurants are required to have them. I loved my times in Rome, although I admit to a decent dose of apprehension upon arrival. After dragging a suitcase along cobbled streets from the station, looking for my hotel with sweat pouring down my face, I eventually found it. After a cool shower, I left to wander the side streets and got lost. I stopped for a gelato advertised at €3 and when left was charged €8. The price increase was attributed to my conduct: I was prompted by the proprietor to sit down while waiting for delivery, but if a seat is taken an additional fee is charged—again, welcome to Rome!

⟶ WEBSITES
italyheaven.co.uk
rome.info
turismoroma.it

All free men, wherever they may live, are citizens of Berlin. And, therefore, as a free man, I take pride in the words "Ich bin ein Berliner."

—John F. Kennedy

⟶ **I'D BEEN GOING TO COLOGNE,** Germany, almost annually for the last twenty years; the location for the world's largest home improvement show takes place there, but I had never been to Berlin. In 2014 I decided to change that. Like many others, I had grown up aware of the wall and the division between East and West Berlin. Upon arrival, the most surprising thing I found in this city of over three million was the lack of evidence of the Berlin Wall. You really have to look for it. The Soviet-built structure separated East and West Berlin for over twenty-eight years and now little remains. Most of it was removed and recycled as street pavement, although tourist shops still sell bits of concrete they claim to be pieces of the wall. (I did not purchase any of these rocks, as there seemed little to authenticate these claims.) I expected to leave Berlin with a firm image of this dividing line; instead I left thinking of the museums, the neighborhoods, the vibrant culture, the busy street scene, and those lovely, tall, well-dressed, somewhat aloof German businessmen—but that is another story.

I love Germany and the German people for their discipline, punctuality, sense of order, and rational, sensible stance. There is also an attractive, quirky side to them, which provides an interesting contrast to all that discipline. I saw formally attired men eating huge ice cream cones in the street at 9 AM; I also saw giant frankfurter sandwiches, bizarre fashion choices, and jugglers and street performers entertaining drivers stopped at red lights. Germany is a safe country for the single woman because it is so disciplined, and Berlin is as safe as the rest of the country. The transit system is great, English is widely spoken, and there is a terrific sense of order. Berlin also has the added advantage of affordability. Compared to many other European cities it is a real bargain, and the weather is rarely extreme, so you can visit any month of the year. With a vibrant arts scene stretching well back over a century (think Cabaret and Marlene Dietrich), an entire island dedicated to museums (there are over 170 museums in Berlin), and a number of distinct neighborhoods to explore, Berlin is a sizable city that offers a lot without breaking the bank.

---> **ARRIVAL**

Transportation is *very* good in Germany—probably the best in the world. The main airport is Tegel, just six kilometers from the center of town. From here a couple of express buses run. The X9 operates every ten minutes to the Zoo Station in West Berlin—a real hub, but, unlike many other European transportation hubs, safe and non-threatening. The TXL runs to Alexanderplatz, the main square in Berlin. The easier option is a cab; at a cost of about €25 from the airport to a centrally located hotel, the trip takes about thirty minutes. Schönefeld Airport is a little farther out, but from here the Airport Express Train runs every thirty minutes and takes thirty minutes to reach central Berlin. A taxi from Schönefeld takes forty-five minutes and will be about €35. If arriving by train at Hauptbahnhof railway station, which is clean and safe, take the S-Bahn subway or a cab to your destination.

> ### ACCOMMODATIONS

The real advantage to Berlin is that it's not an expensive place to stay, compared to many other European cities such as Paris, London, or Rome. Book a hotel that has breakfast; this is usually a buffet with a great array of fresh breads, yogurt, fruit, meat and cheeses, and sometimes hot offerings. Many hotels are in wonderful historical buildings, and as transportation is safe at every hour (I returned to my hotel at 12:30 AM and was amazed at how many people, and not just the under-twenty-fives, were out at that hour). Booking accommodations away from the city center and using transit is an option. I stayed in Kreuzberg, which offers an alternative local scene with small streets and cafés. Charlottenburg is a bit smarter than Kreuzberg and has more options. Most of the larger business hotels are located around Mitte, which is in the city's historical and shopping district—ideal if you want to be in the center of things.

Berlin is big. It has a reliable, easy, safe, accessible public transport system. Because it sprawls, become acquainted with it to take full advantage of what is on offer. Take the number 100 and 200 buses, as both pass major tourist attractions; this easy, cheap option acquaints the newly arrived visitor with the city. Although it is possible to spend every day walking, Berlin is really a place to see by area; at least three or four days are needed to even begin to scratch the surface, more if you plan to spend time in the wonderful museums. Mitte is the main area with the Brandenburg Gate, libraries, opera, galleries, and shopping. Along with the world-renowned attractions (Brandenburg Gate, Checkpoint Charlie, Tiergarten), the highlights of my visit included a tour of the new parliament building, Reichstag, which has great views of the city; admission is free but you need to book a time in advance. Museumsinsel (Museum Island) is a UNESCO World Heritage Site where it is easy to spend an entire day getting lost in the history and art. In contrast, the East Side Gallery is the one kilometer of wall remaining, although there are also tall column-type pieces remaining around the city. The tourist office is located at Alexanderplatz, which also has toilets. The recently opened Jewish Museum is an architecturally impressive building with weird sloping floors and a quirky layout displays the shocking stories of the Jewish community and is well worth a visit. Finally, when fatigue takes over, try the Spree River cruise to rest tired limbs, or consider renting a bike, as the cycle trails are well laid out and easy to follow.

→ ADDITIONAL INFORMATION
Berlin is as safe as it is economical, and as long as you do not mind the cold it can be visited at any time of the year. If temperatures do plummet, visit KaDeWe, the largest department store in Europe with a staff of over two thousand and an inventory of over forty thousand items, or shop on the famous Kurfürstendamm. Another distinct advantage is that Berlin is not overrun with tourists. Being there involves mixing with Berliners, not just visitors, and as Kennedy acknowledged, in a sense we are all Berliners. As many European cities grow in popularity, it's refreshing to visit a city that retains a natural charm and is not a complete tourist trap. Berlin is a very desirable European location for the single woman, and at the risk of repeating myself, it is very, very safe. If time and agenda oblige, consider taking one of the super-efficient trains to another European city such as Vienna, Prague, Cologne, or Budapest; they are all easily accessible. Enjoy!

→ WEBSITES

berlin-tourist-information.de

berlin.angloinfo.com

berlin.de

visitberlin.de

Barcelona is a very old city in which you can feel the weight of history; it is haunted by history. You cannot walk around it without perceiving it.

—Carlos Ruiz Zafón

⟶ **WITH FIVE KILOMETERS OF BEACH** within easy access of the city center, Barcelona is the European city where you'll see topless girls sunbathing one moment while taking in architectural sightseeing the next. When I visited early in June there were women of every age topless on the beaches. I was a rarity in my one-piece, feeling very much the matronly prude as my Spanish sisters strutted their large, swinging stuff with an unbridled confidence I envied. It's liberating to see real female bodies of every age and size exposed and to realize (yet again) how the advertising industry and media in general regularly skew our perception.

Barcelona is a great city to visit and explore but does have a reputation for petty theft and crime. I've visited on three different occasions and have not been a victim, but every guidebook warns tourists that pick-pocketing and bag snatching are epidemic, problematic, frequent, severe, and the worst of every major European city. As a large city with over four million people in the area, high youth unemployment, and a lot of tourists, the stage is set for crime, so if nervously considering a first trip to Europe, Barcelona may not be the perfect spot; choose Berlin, Vienna, Edinburgh, or Budapest instead. But if you have confidence and want to visit one of the most vibrant cities in Europe and practice your street smarts, I see no reason not to vacation in this wonderful city, which has a unique 'round-the-clock energy. And you will not be alone. Barcelona—famous for Gaudí and his Catalan architecture and artists such as Salvador Dalí, Pablo Picasso, and Joan Miró—is a very popular weekend destination for many Europeans as it has so much to offer: Gothic squares, beaches, a vibrant party atmosphere, and lots of bars, restaurants, and music venues. Very much a party town—the action starts at around 9 PM and carries on until daybreak—Barcelona is the fourth most-visited European city, after Paris, London, and Rome.

---⟶ ARRIVAL

Flying to Barcelona from North America will inevitably involve having to take a connecting flight within Europe (in London, Paris, Frankfurt, or Amsterdam) so the journey to Barcelona's airport, El Prat (which is in the municipality of El Prat de Llogbregat) will be long. Reach central Barcelona by taking the airport train service to the main Barcelona Sants station (less than €4), which takes about twenty minutes, or the Aerobus (€6). Both these options will mean arriving tired and disoriented, and will also mean that you end up walking with luggage, perhaps along narrow back streets, to find accommodations. With this in mind, and with the knowledge that Barcelona's more unsavory characters target newly arrived tourists, invest in a cab (€30–€40) from the airport. While more expensive than mass public transport alternatives, I believe the jet-lagged lady needs to make this investment in this city.

⟶ ACCOMMODATIONS

During visits to Barcelona, I have stayed in a noisy, cheap, centrally located small hotel, in a somewhat anemic, impersonal, corporate-type hotel (which offered good weekend rates but was away from the night life and attractions), and about forty kilometers out of town in the small seaside town of Sitges. Although away from the city, Sitges is on a direct rail link to Barcelona. If I return, I'll want to stay in Sitges again. One of the joys of Barcelona is the available accommodations options. Compared with other European cities, hotels here are not that pricey, but again location is key. Hotels adjacent to Las Ramblas are the most expensive and could be noisy. Sant Pere and La Ribera are good options, centrally located, and have some designer boutique options. Avoid Barri Gòtic and El Raval, which, although central, have few tourists and are reported to be not that safe. While there is a star rating, these ratings can be misleading, so read the reviews from other tourists before making a commitment. Barcelona's low season is from November to April (excluding Christmas) when prices fall to match the temperatures.

Central Barcelona is a relatively easy city to navigate, with most of the major tourist sites within easy walking distance of each other. The Old City has wonderfully preserved buildings and you can easily pass a couple of days ticking these off your itinerary. The primary attraction is Las Rambla, a large pedestrian boulevard full of cafés, flower stores, and sculptures, with a river of people flowing for over a kilometer toward the sea. But remember, it's also a haven for pick-pockets. Visiting at 9 AM is totally different from visiting at 9 PM, so try to do both. Las Rambla, together with La Catedral, architecture by Gaudí, and works by artists such as Dali and Picasso, are all here to explore. The top two tourists' sites are the Picasso Museum and Antoni Gaudí's Sagrada Familia Church. Both these venues, and the Casa Mila, should be booked in advance to avoid disappointment. While as a single woman I enjoyed my ventures to these and other central tourist spots, I can also highly recommend two other excursions: first, take a train ride out to the vast monastery of Montserrat, forty kilometers northwest of the city; you can not only tour the monastery buildings nestled among the craggy rocks, but also walk in the surrounding countryside on a number of clearly defined footpaths. Here there are splendid views, and it's a great place to spend a day after crowded sightseeing in Barcelona. Also, it's safe; the pick-pockets do not make the effort to take the trip. Opt for the public train, which is easy and reasonable, and not the organized tour. Second, a trip to Sitges, a perfect seaside town with narrow cobbled streets, is just a thirty-minute train ride from the city.

Rick Steves, the famous US travel writer, believes tourists are more likely to be pick-pocketed in Barcelona (particularly at Las Rambla) than anywhere else in Europe. And a number of other travel writers echo his opinions on how the subways are another venue for pick-pockets. Given their concerns, I thought long and hard about including Barcelona in this book and chose to do so because I have had such positive experiences there, especially outside of the city. I was not a victim and for the most part felt safe. Barcelona does not offer just one vacation but can be the base for many adventures. Yes, perhaps street smarts are needed here more than elsewhere, but if you're prepared it is a highly desirable location. The biggest problem I found was the number of tourists. When I visited in my twenties, there were not the crowds there are today, and it was this, not the crime issue, that diluted my high opinion of the place. Finally, let me end on my favorite subject: restrooms. They are not plentiful. When you find one, visit it.

⎯⎯➤ **WEBSITES**

barcelona-tourist-guide.com
barcelona.com
barcelonaturisme.com
spain.info

BRUSSELS

Take Flight for

CHOCOLATE
DAY TRIPS
HOTELS

In Brussels everything is easy. It is not a very big city and the people are quiet and warm.

—Eric-Emmanuel Schmitt

⟶ **IF ASKED TO NAME THE** major tourist attraction in Brussels, most people would be at a loss. It does not have an Eiffel Tower, a Buckingham Palace, or a Colosseum—but it *does* have a statue of a little boy peeing. Beyond that, Brussels has the best chocolate in the world, sold, it seems, at every corner. Brussels is at the center of the European Parliament, has a Flemish/French/German-influenced culture, and has an ambiance that is delightful for the single woman. It is also a great location from which to explore other European cities, such as Amsterdam, Paris, and Bruges. Most of the attractions in Brussels lie within the Pentagon—a ring road—making the city easy to navigate. Unlike in most other European cities, in Brussels it is cheaper to stay in a four-star hotel in the center of town in July and August and over weekends than at other times, as this is when the business clique moves out. Although not cheap, Brussels offers more accommodations indulgences than other European hot spots.

⟶ ARRIVAL

Brussels Airport (also called Brussels National or Brussels-Zaventem) is located eleven kilometers northeast of Brussels, in Zaventem. Although travelers can take direct flights from North America, most that come from there land in London or Amsterdam. Trains operate from the airport to the city center and take fifteen minutes (at a cost of about €5). Taxis offer door-to-door services, of course, but are considerably more expensive at around €40. Be warned: the traffic in Brussels is brutal, so taxi rides can be long. Three train stations serve the city: Central, Nord, and Midi. Trains for international destinations arrive at Gare de Midi. Train travel is great, although it can be expensive for international connections, especially on Eurostar, unless you book in advance. Train travel to other beautiful Belgian towns (Bruges, Antwerp, Ghent) is easy and more reasonable.

⟶ ACCOMMODATIONS

Because much of the work of the European Parliament takes place in Brussels, it has large business-oriented hotels that empty over weekends and in July and August. Therefore, with a little bit of planning, the solo woman traveler on a budget can enjoy luxurious four-star rooms, as prices can drop by as much as

50 percent below advertised rates. Make sure to book at a hotel within the Old City to be close to attractions; after a hard day of walking, exploring, and devouring chocolate, you can easily return to luxurious surroundings to recover. A number of newer business hotels are adjacent to the Parliament, but these are far out of the center. A star rating is used to classify establishments, with one star being very basic. Choose hotels with a rating greater than three stars if you want a reasonable level of comfort. As with other European hotels, rooms in establishments full of character are often small. Booking in advance is advised (although you may get real bargains for last-minute rooms if you can cope with the stress of not having booked a bed for the night). There are wonderful street cafés, so choosing a hotel that offers breakfast is not necessary; most have great buffets.

⟶ ACTIVITIES

Although busy, I find Brussels to be less tourist dominated than other European cities such as London, Paris, and Barcelona. The single woman who wants to acquaint herself with European culture, explore primarily by walking without getting too lost, consume the best chocolate on earth, and make easy train connections to other wonderful Belgian cities will be well satisfied with a holiday here. Two to three days is all you need to explore and appreciate the city. Every tourist starts with the Grand Place—Brussels' main square, which is more like an outdoor museum as everywhere you look there is another statue, gargoyle, window, or door to admire. Numerous cafés and restaurants are positioned around the square and are good for refreshments and people watching. From this starting point you can easily access other buildings of interest, such as the

Town Hall, City Museum (one of over seventy-five museums in the city), and four of the more famous chocolate shops. This is the main tourist spot, but by exiting the square and exploring the back streets, you can find more chocolate shops as well as a multitude of interesting streets and alleys. After exploring Brussels, take a trip to Bruges, which is less than an hour away by train and offers some of the most beautiful buildings in Europe. Bruges is centered in a very compact one square kilometer. It is very, very touristy but has great architecture, shopping, and eating. Don't expect to be alone—it's crowded but beautiful. The Belgian city of Ghent is only thirty minutes away by train, and while not as famous or pretty as Bruges, is less touristy and for the North American woman continues to entertain with stunning architecture. The excellent train system has a senior rate offering 50 percent off travel at non-peak times.

—→ ADDITIONAL INFORMATION

Although in this book I do not focus on travel as a way to meet the opposite sex, I have to acknowledge there is something uniquely sexy about Belgian men; they dress as well as the French, are as polite as the Germans, and are far more sophisticated in amorous advances than Italians or Spaniards. In my experience, Belgian men are more flirtatious, friendlier, fitter, and far better looking than most other European men. This finding is based only on my (limited) research and is not something touted by the Belgium Tourist Board, but is another reason, in addition to everything outlined above, to pay the country a visit. Belgium is a safe place for women to visit and has a low crime rate compared to many other cities of a comparative size, but as with all tourist destinations, petty crime does occur. Using public transportation at any time of the day is generally safe as is walking the streets in the evening. However, one of the most disturbing things for me was encountering women, with young children at their side, asking for money, which for some reason seems more prevalent here than in other European cities. (I also experienced this in my last visit to Seattle, so perhaps it is just a sign of our times.)

Belgium is known not only for chocolate but also for beer. Home to over three hundred different brews, my favorites are those infused with fruits such as strawberries and cherries—very refreshing, but be prepared: sometimes the alcohol content is much higher than we on this side of the Atlantic are accustomed to. Try drinking Belgian beer as you sit outside one of the many interesting bars, under a heat lamp and wrapped in the blanket provided. Waffles topped with fruit, cream, and chocolate are a constant temptation as are the pomme frites (fries); tantalizing street food is everywhere. Although there are three official languages (French, Flemish, and German), everyone speaks English and the euro is the currency used. In summary, this is a great European center to explore and to explore from. For anyone who has not traveled to Europe before, it's a very sensible first-time choice.

———→ **WEBSITES**
brussels.info
brusselsinternational.be
visitbelgium.com
visitbrussels.be

Amsterdam has more than 150 canals and 1,250 bridges, but it never seems crowded.

—Julie Burchill

⟶ **I HAVE BEEN TO AMSTERDAM** four times in my life, the first time as a student in the late 1970s when it was rather run down and famous for the drug culture and red light district. Over the years a renaissance has occurred; now the red light district is difficult to distinguish from the rest of the city, especially during the day, and the entire place is safe for the single woman to explore. The best part of Amsterdam is the stunning historical streetscape: tall, slim, corniced houses, every one different from its neighbor, positioned parallel to canals on tree-lined cobblestone streets . . . enchanting.

Amsterdam is neither too big nor too small, but just right. Within two days of arrival, getting lost should not be an issue. I find it less trendy than other European cities such as London and Paris; there are fewer designer-clad gals prancing around to make you feel inadequate in your Josef Seibel flat sandals and sensible Tilly Endurable attire. Amsterdam has real people in it. And each one of the residents owns at least one bike, probably more—bikes are everywhere.

If there is one disadvantage, it must be the popularity of this European city; consequently, the crowds at certain times of the year can be extensive. In 2014 over eight million people visited the city, with the peak months being July and August, something to consider when planning a trip. But Amsterdam does not need to be bathed in sunshine to be appreciated; it is a stunning place in the cold and rain for the well-prepared solo woman, especially as a great deal of time will probably be spent in the galleries and museums, away from the elements. I much prefer to cope with a bit of rain rather than hordes of tourists.

⟶ ARRIVAL

Just as North America has a number of hub airports (Dallas, Chicago, Houston), so does Europe (Frankfurt, London's Heathrow), and Amsterdam is one of these hubs. (When you're leaving Amsterdam, make sure you have enough time to access the multitude of stores in its airport; North American international departure terminals and many in Europe are not half as good as Amsterdam's.) Many charter and scheduled airlines fly directly to Amsterdam Schiphol Airport from major cities in the USA and Canada, so although the transatlantic flight is long, the direct connection is a real bonus. Train services to Amsterdam's city center and the main train station operate every ten minutes from the airport terminal between 6 AM and 12:30 at night and cost a mere €4. Take this option then catch a taxi to your hotel; this works out to be far cheaper than a taxi from the airport to central Amsterdam, which can be €40 to €50 if the traffic is bad (and it often is very bad). On that note, no one in their right mind should consider driving in central Amsterdam.

⟶ ACCOMMODATIONS

Among the advantages of Amsterdam not being a large city are the ease of finding suitable accommodations in the center of things and not having to use transit during a stay. While at first glance hotels in the famous Dam Square vicinity may be appealing, be aware that Amsterdam does have a vibrant night life, especially during weekends, and choosing a hotel in this busy central sector with loud street noise and the adjacent bars operating well into the early hours of the morning may not prove conducive to a good night's sleep. My suggestion is to select accommodations in the Canal Ring or Museum Quarter. As at many European hotels, rooms and bathrooms tend to be much smaller than those in North America, sometimes in establishments that do not have elevators. Make sure to read the small print when booking; digest the guest reviews or you may find your room is on the fifth floor of an eighteenth-century establishment without an elevator or air conditioning. Anything rated three or more stars should be fine. Finding a hotel offering breakfast is not important, as hundreds of great cafés and gorgeous bakeries in Amsterdam will satisfy any early-morning cravings. Leave your hotel and follow the smell to find breakfast. As mentioned above, a number of tourists flock here in the summer and room rates reflect this—another reason to travel in the quieter months.

During my most recent four-day trip to Amsterdam, I settled into a pleasant daily routine of walking and exploring until about 3 PM, then taking a canal trip for an hour or two to rest my aching legs (Amsterdam has more canals than Venice.) After this respite, I wandered back to the hotel as the light faded, observing the bars as daytime clientele turned to night-time clientele. As I meandered, I explored the many small shops and boutiques, which were open well into the evening hours. While there is some repetition in the canal tours, views from the water offer a different perspective of the city's architecture, and the narrative offered is a relaxing way to learn about the city and is often more diverse and easier to absorb than information provided in guidebooks. Some of these canal tours journey away from the city center into quieter and more industrial neighborhoods of the city, offering a view that one doesn't get when strolling. As Amsterdam is famous for waterways, taking a canal tour should be a key activity, as should visiting a selection of the over forty museums and 140 art galleries on offer. Recently the Docklands area has been developed, housing a number of avant-garde architectural statements. Street markets of varying size can also be found, frequently when they are least expected, adding to the magical, unpredictable character of the city. The flower market is a must-see. You can easily explore Amsterdam in three to four days and, if you have more time to travel, you can use it as a base for rail connections to other European wonders such as Bruges, Paris, and Brussels. Many of Amsterdam's most famous attractions—Anne Frank House, Van Gogh Museum, and Rijksmuseum, to name a few—need to be booked in advance to assure entry.

Do not think traveling to Holland will require a crash course in speaking Dutch—everyone speaks English; every café and restaurant menu is in English; bus and tram drivers speak it fluently; even when you're wandering the streets, English is the prominent language you'll hear. As a large European city, Amsterdam does experience petty crime, and tourists can be targeted, but it is not any more dangerous than other European centers of population. One of the best times to explore Amsterdam is Sunday morning, when things are quieter and fewer people are around; later on in the day, and especially on weekends in the summer, there are often live music concerts. As always, it is these unexpected events not in the guidebooks or on any planned agenda that can be the most memorable. I found the most dangerous and stressful things about Amsterdam are the bicycles and their operators. As a tourist, it's too easy to drift into the bike lanes or cross at an intersection and not watch for bikes. Many of these bikes look as if they have been in service since the nineteenth century, and frequently accommodate more than one person (often a child) who is precariously positioned on the antique while the operator steers one-handed and speaks on a cell phone. Likewise, trams are almost silent and it is very easy to walk into the tram lanes while looking up at the wonderful architecture, leading me to suspect the accident and emergency department of the local Amsterdam hospital is full of tourists injured by the city's vehicles. And so my greatest word of caution is to be alert when walking.

——→ **WEBSITES**

amsterdaminfo.com
dutchamsterdam.nl
holland.com
iamsterdam.info

BUDAPEST

Take Flight for

SPAS
SAFETY
EASTERN EUROPEAN
CULTURE

Budapest is a prime site for dreamers: the East's exuberant vision of the West, the West's uneasy hallucination of the East. It is a dreamed-up city.

—M. John Harrison

⟶ **IF ONE WORD SUMS UP** Budapest, it's "safe." This wonderful Eastern European city is full of gorgeous buildings, huge architectural masterpieces (mostly built within the last two hundred years) with statues, gargoyles, and magnificent huge wooden doors, all of which invite you to explore without any threat of aggressive panhandlers, money changers, pick-pockets, and vagrants. There seems to be little disorder here: no street crime, no litter, no drunken youth on the street, no rude drivers shouting at the lost tourist. This is a city made for the mature single female traveler. Another key advantage (which will not last for long) is the comparative lack of tourists. Budapest does not suffer from crowds as London, Paris, Amsterdam, and Barcelona do, making it a delight to explore. I spent four wonderful days here (but needed a week), and after each day exploring a spa beckoned. Viking River Cruises boats stop here, but, in stark contrast to other European centers, there are very few Asian tourists on organized bus tours and few American visitors with matching backpacks and identity labels around their necks. Expect this to change, but in the meantime enjoy a city destined to become the next European hot spot.

⟶ **ARRIVAL**

Flying to Budapest from North America is a two-stage process involving a stop in the UK, Germany, Holland, or another European hub airport. Consequently, getting here takes more travel time than a trip to London, Amsterdam, or Paris. But once you arrive, life is easy: from the baggage claim area in the airport a bright orange strip painted on the floor directs passengers to the shuttle bus kiosk, where for about $20 (2015 price) a shuttle bus will take the weary traveler directly to a hotel, or any other location in central Budapest. The disadvantage of this service is the bus accommodates eight people, so sometimes the bus does not depart until all seats are filled; this means you could be the last passenger to be dropped off. (I don't think this is a real disadvantage—you get to see the city as the bus tours to different hotels). This is a reliable, safe mode of transportation and a great alternative to the taxi, which costs significantly more. The airport is about a twenty-minute drive from the center of town. I arrived at 10:30 PM and had only a fifteen-minute wait until the bus departed, which meant I was in bed before midnight.

I stayed in November when the weather was supposed to be cold, but it was not (writes the menopausal woman). There were very few visitors, so my four-star hotel at a great central location cost under $60 a night (2015 price), including a hot buffet breakfast. Select a hotel with breakfast; unlike other European cities, Budapest does not offer a wide range of breakfast choices. The city is divided into two sections, Buda and Pest, which were once separate cities on different sides of the Danube. I advise staying in the Pest section, which is closer to the shopping and many of the main activities. As the city has only recently been discovered as a tourist destination, some of the more reasonable hotels may be more basic than many North American tourists expect, so if you opt for a three-star hotel, be prepared for a few rough edges. Even my four-star hotel had only one English-language TV station and a dubious, rattling elevator, which accounted for the only stressful experience during my entire time in the city.

───→ ACTIVITIES

Unlike many other European cities where booking in advance and lining up to see the main sights are the order of the day, as yet these pressures are not the norm in Budapest. For the most part you can see what you want, when you want, without standing in line with hundreds of others. It's a great city to walk around, and after a couple of days relying on the map and getting lost, you'll get a good understanding of the geography. Budapest sits atop 80 to 120 active springs and wells from which seventy million tons of water flow, so there are a number of spa baths, the most famous being Szechenyi Spa (which has thirteen different pools, three of them outside). This should be on everyone's to-do list. It's huge—go at dusk, sit in the warm water, and watch the stars appear in the sky as the locals play chess and the tourists get lost. Gellert Spa, with lion-faced gargoyles spurting water, is also good and easier to get to, as it's more centrally located. When you enter these spas, the logistics of finding where to get changed and what to do with your clothes is a bit of a test, but worth it.

Also, I recommend you see an opera, even if you're not a fan. Tickets are priced from $10, and everyone attending gets dressed up, making it an ideal people-watching place. I stayed for only two acts (opera is not my thing) but was impressed to see five young men in their twenties sitting in front of me, having a night out together while fully engaged in the performance. I could never imagine my teenage sons suggesting to their friends they go to see opera.

Walk everywhere, especially on the banks of the Danube, or take the number 2 tram that runs along the banks of this famous river. Bus tickets must be purchased in advance from the large transportation stations. Walking at night and in the early evening is not a problem, and street markets often have live music to make your return to your accommodations a delight. Finally, pay a visit to the huge, two-tiered covered market to purchase gifts for people at home, or to simply get a taste of Hungarian culture.

⟶ ADDITIONAL INFORMATION

Budapest is catching up with other European cities when competing for tourist dollars, and while this is currently an advantage for those of us who dislike crowds, there are a few limitations. Budapest has limited international cuisine (i.e., there are few Chinese, Indian, Mexican, or Japanese restaurants or pubs, and only a couple of Starbucks, but I expect this to change); the local currency, the Hungarian forint (or HUF), is extensively used, as is the euro, but while the city is responding to the growth of tourism (e.g., all employees in the service industry speak English), the Hungarians, though polite, are not overly friendly and seem a little aloof or formal. Make sure to keep 200 forint in change on hand; this is the fee charged by the (generally) large, stern-faced women dressed in white uniforms guarding the entrance to the restrooms. Speaking of restrooms, you have to seek them out. Even public places, such as museums and the Parliament building, charge for use. Still, they are well kept. To do Budapest justice, especially if you plan to visit the vast array of galleries, museums, and spas, plan to spend a week. In summer, a boat trip between Vienna and Budapest takes a few hours, so consider visiting other European cities (Vienna and Prague are easily accessible from Budapest). In summary, I found Budapest fascinating; it made me feel special and not simply one of the crowd. This is why, of all the cities listed in this book, it is the first I wish to return to.

——> WEBSITES
budapest.com
discoverbudapest.com
visitbudapest.travel

PRAGUE

Take Flight for

SQUARES
COBBLED STREETS
TOURISTS

Prague is the Paris of the Nineties.

—Marion Ross

→ **PRAGUE (PRAHA) WINS MY PRIZE** for being *the* most confusing to navigate. I spent four days here and walked each day from 9 AM until 6 to 7 PM and still could not ascertain the layout; I kept finding myself not where I expected to be and was often confused. The signposts are numerous but all in Czech. The roads are cobblestone and twisting, and just when you think you know where you are, confusion strikes. The river horseshoes around the city and appears and reappears where not expected. Don't get me wrong—it's a great, gorgeous, architecturally stunning city to get lost in . . . but be warned, getting lost is very easy to do.

Prague has become *the* place to visit, and in the space of twenty-five years after the fall of communism it has successfully marketed itself to the world. Especially on weekends the population swells, as the city is also becoming known for stag/bachelor and hen parties. Souvenir shops are everywhere, as are tourists; there are a gazillion places to eat and even more in which to drink; everyone speaks English. If you decide to go when the weather is good, expect hordes of tourists and inflated prices. In 2013 over seven million people visited Prague. I visited in November when it was cold but not crowded, so I have a bit of a love/hate relationship with this city. The architecture and the buildings are truly wonderful, unscathed by the bombing and resultant damage that afflicted many other European cities during the Second World War. It's a great place to explore, which I love, but it's completely geared toward the tourist, more so than London or Paris. Because Prague is more compact, tourism is concentrated, which I don't love. There is little "real" Prague left; although the buildings are breathtaking and the cobbled streets iconic, edifices are occupied by Costa Coffee, Zara, and tourist emporiums, and the roads are crowded with money changers and tour guides. Only when I took a bus out of town to the airport did I feel I was actually encountering anything like the real (non-tourist) Prague.

⟶ ARRIVAL

The airport is relatively small and easy to navigate—however, taxis can be difficult to find and the drivers have a reputation for inflating prices. The guidebooks recommend using only taxis positioned in an official, government-designated taxi rank. A more reasonable option is to take the airport shuttle bus; it leaves every thirty minutes and takes about thirty minutes to reach downtown, where a good metro system provides delivery to your destination. Alternatively, the number 19 bus from the airport takes about twenty minutes to reach the Dejvická metro station (on the green line) where you can then take a subway to downtown. It works out to be under $5. Numerous travel guides warn of pick-pockets and other unsavory characters. While it is always good to be vigilant, none of the transportation hubs seemed particularly threatening and I found these warnings to be exaggerated. Be prepared: every street is cobblestone, so the wheels of your suitcase will take a beating if your hotel is a few blocks away from the transportation hub. (By the way, stiletto heels get stuck between cobblestones—another good reason to leave them at home).

→ ACCOMMODATIONS

In 2015, my four-star, centrally located hotel came with a hot buffet breakfast and complimentary wine in the evening, all for $60—but it was November. The Vltava River runs through Prague (Praha), so you can choose two areas for accommodations: the quieter Castle District (which has smaller hotels, many on steep inclines) or the Old Town. My advice is to opt for the Old Town, where there are greater choices. Accommodations can be pricey during the peak season, which is between June and August, and not all offer air conditioning. Book in advance— demand is heavy. Remember, the room could be five hundred years old, so check out the small print to ensure there is heating and/or air conditioning, as well as elevators and Wi-Fi. Prague gets very cold during the winter months, so if you're visiting then, take warm clothes to fend off the chill.

The key is to wander and get lost, consult a map, relocate, and wander again and get lost. On the first full day in the city, do this in the Old Town area; on the second day, cross the river via the famous Charles Bridge and do it in the Castle District and Little Quarter. You can repeat this pattern on subsequent days. Take one of the bus or walking tours (young people are everywhere with umbrellas advertising these tours) to obtain some rudimentary understanding of the labyrinth that is Prague. Comfy walking shoes and a decent map are of paramount importance. Follow the maze of streets to the key tourist attractions, but do not get too concerned if you miss them, or if it takes longer to access them than planned—inevitably you'll discover others, as it is quite a compact city. On my second morning in Prague, I spent ninety minutes trying to find the famous Charles Street Bridge, which turned out to be a brief ten-minute walk from my hotel. The St. Nicolas Church area and the Castle District are easier to navigate than the Old Town, which has many small streets and all the shops. If you feel like you want some culture or to take a break from walking, many classical concerts are on offer. Public transportation in the form of the metro is good.

──→ **ADDITIONAL INFORMATION**

The Czech crown (koruna) is still the main unit of currency, although the euro is also widely accepted. Restrooms are clean and well signposted and guarded by formidable women who demand payment, so keep a supply of change on hand. If shopping is on the agenda, and not just for souvenirs, there are numerous shops ready to tempt, but they tend to be the same chain stores found in every large city (Zara, Benetton, the Levi's Store, Louis Vuitton, H&M, C&A, Marks and Spencer, etc.).

Starbucks, McDonalds, and Costa Coffee are common but are interspersed with some wonderful local restaurants, street markets, cake shops, and bars. Before I visited Prague, a number of guidebooks warned of petty theft by individuals wanting to change money. While I was approached on a couple of occasions, this was not an issue. A polite "No thank you" and a brisk walk away were all that was needed. Overall the city seemed very safe, probably because of the number of visitors, all just as lost as me.

While I would not deter anyone from visiting, my biggest problem with the city is its own success; it's almost "Disneyland-ish." I was one of millions of tourists and did not feel that my experience was my own. Everything is geared to the tourist. Consider visiting Prague in addition to Budapest, Vienna, or Berlin, all of which are easily accessible by train (book in advance and travel first class). All these cities accommodate their own citizens as well as tourists and, in my opinion, offer a far more genuine picture of European culture. In other cities, I did not feel like one of a vast number of tourists. In Prague I was very much one of the crowd. I suppose I find Prague to be like the designer girl in high school—the one who had everything, but no matter how hard I tried I never understood what made her tick or what others saw in her. I have included Prague because of the international reputation it has; I am happy to have visited, but unlike most of the other places detailed in this book, I have no strong desire to return.

———> **WEBSITES**

prague-information.eu
prague-tourist-information.com
prague.eu
pragueexperience.com

VIENNA

Take Flight for

CHATEAUX
GATEAUX
MUSIC

Vienna is a handsome, lively city and pleases me
exceedingly.
—Frédéric Chopin

⟶ **THIS IS THE PLACE FOR** palaces. A visit to Vienna (Wein)
not only allows city exploration but within easy reach are huge,
lavish chateaux with hundreds of rooms and extensive gardens,
all easily and safely accessible. Therefore, in contrast to many
other European destinations, Vienna allows the aspiring queen
to access the homes of the very, very rich with little effort and
provides an alternative to city center exploration. And Vienna
is so safe, so secure, so easy to walk around, so welcoming, has
so many gateaux and so much culture. Everyone is polite, waits
for green lights before crossing the road, and apologizes if they

bump into you. The streets are clean, the traffic predictable, and the accommodations wonderful, making Vienna *the* easiest place for the North American girl to be alone. And should you get lonely, sad, or just hungry, there are hundreds of cafés and restaurants offering the best rich creamy desserts in the world, guaranteed to immediately make you a happier (and heavier) being. As the capital of Austria, Vienna is one of Europe's most welcoming cities. There's a dearth of big skyscrapers and ugly buildings, an abundance of delightful parks, and a great opera and concert scene. Mozart, although born in Salzberg, is reputed to have preferred Vienna, and the Viennese tourist board has been enthusiastic to promote this. If you appreciate paintings, music, architecture, opera, and creamy desserts, this is the place to be.

ARRIVAL

Direct flights from North America are not numerous, so arriving in Vienna will (for most people) involve a connection through a European hub such as London, Frankfurt, or Amsterdam. Although this route is long, access to central Vienna (once at the airport) is amazingly easy and affordable. Vienna's (Wein) main airport is Schwechat, nineteen kilometers south of the city. The pristine airport train (CAT) takes a nonstop route from the airport to the center of town in fifteen minutes (€9). Take a taxi to the hotel from here or take the S-Bahn. Although taxis are available at €40 from the airport (with a journey time of thirty minutes), there seems little point in incurring this expense. Vienna has excellent train connections to destinations in the rest of Europe and within Austria. You can also travel between cities by boat in the summer months and sail down the Danube.

→ ACCOMMODATIONS

While anything but cheap, Vienna has a wide array of accommodations, from newer designer chic boutique hotels, to large chain establishments, to smaller budget alternatives. Many of the smaller hotels occupy the most stunning historical buildings. Most of the accommodations are within the Innere Stadt (inner city); the most central options are the most expensive and have a greater star rating. Hotels outside the central area are more reasonable and a reliable option, as the transportation system is good, cheap, and very safe. Booking ahead is recommended and, if staying in the summer months, ensure there is air conditioning. Generally the hotels provide good buffet breakfasts; booking a hotel without this option means seeking out coffee and gateaux will be the first activity on your daily agenda—but really, is there any better way to start a day?

→ ACTIVITIES

While it is possible to appreciate numerous cultural and historical high points of the city within three days, if you plan to explore some of the many palaces (and you should), which can easily be reached by the subway system, five days is the minimum time needed. The main museums and cultural buildings are within the Innere Stadt. A UNESCO-protected area ranked as one of the ten largest cultural complexes in the world, it includes the Hofburg Palace, the must-see venue in the city.

Walking in Vienna is a delight, and with every corner turned it seems there are more wonderful places to enthrall. The Vienna Card (which you can purchase at your hotel, the Vienna Transportation System sales offices and information booths, or the Vienna Tourist Information Center) provides seventy-two hours of discounts on travel to museums and restaurants. The tram service circles the inner ring road, giving you an opportunity to become acquainted with the city while taking in great views of the buildings. The Opera House offers reasonably priced last-minute tickets (to ensure entrance, book in advance).

A number of Vienna highlights will live in my memory forever: the Hofburg Imperial Palace with its massive rooms, gardens, and squares; visiting the Palace Belvedere early one morning in June and pretending I owned the place while no one else was around; the Leopold Museum, which has artist Gustav Klimt's famous painting "The Kiss," and while reproductions of his work on tea towels, mugs, key chains, etc. are sold everywhere in the city, it is better to see the original. I took the U-Bahn to the yellow-painted Schloss Schonbrunn to see this seventeenth-century, two-hundred-room imperial palace (only forty rooms are open to the public; to ensure access, book in advance). But the biggest highlight was eating the gateaux and gelatos in the multitude of cafés, and not being asked to share. Although I never tend to return to the same place, I discovered a lovely open-air establishment in a large cobblestone square opposite the Spanish riding school and visited on four consecutive days.

⟶ ADDITIONAL INFORMATION

The truly lovely thing about being a single woman in Vienna is the total ease of this foreign city. It is completely non-threatening; everyone speaks English; toilets are clean and plentiful. I even heard a story about how the city played classical music in the subway as a way of successfully deterring drug activity. It is a great city for walking but also for biking, especially around the (flat) Ring Road and City Park, and has a designated bike path and bike share program. While I am not brave enough to cycle in London, Amsterdam, or Paris, I had no problem hiring a bike for a couple of hours here. In summary, if you've never been to Europe and are looking for an easy, safe place to visit, Vienna is that place. And with easy train connections to Berlin, Budapest, and Prague, more European cities can be added to an itinerary. Finally, before (or after) a visit, watch the 1949 black-and-white film *The Third Man*, set in Vienna, starring Orson Wells, and featuring some of the most iconic movie scenes ever shot.

→ **WEBSITES**

aboutvienna.org
vienna.info
wien.info.en

This is a city of shifting light, of changing skies, of sudden vistas. A city so beautiful it breaks the heart again and again.

—Alexander McCall Smith

⟶ **EACH YEAR, FROM THE AGE** of ten, and until she died in 1983, I visited my grandmother who lived not far from this fairy tale city. Edinburgh is dominated by a huge gray castle on a rock looming above the city itself, and is known as "the Athens of the north." My grandparents lived between Edinburgh and Glasgow, so I got to know both cities. I preferred Edinburgh then and still do. This city of five hundred thousand is the second-most popular tourist destination in Britain after London and has all the touristy paraphernalia you would expect from a city proudly displaying its Scottish roots. Bagpipe-playing buskers, an abundance of tartan, whiskey-tasting emporiums, kilts representing every clan, and furry highland cattle stuffed toys are all proudly displayed at every opportunity.

All the clichés that we associate with Scotland and the Scottish are here, but it is not at all tacky or cheap. Edinburgh is sophisticated, charming, and very friendly. Characterized by large, gray stone buildings, home to the seat of the Scottish Parliament, and famous for the Edinburgh Festival (which takes place in August each year), Edinburgh has lost some of the rough edges that were part of its culture when I first visited. In the last forty years I have seen it become a chic, sophisticated city with an ever-growing arts and culture scene. World-famous authors such as JK Rowling, Alexander McCall Smith, and Ian Rankin have been instrumental in promoting its charms. Edinburgh is easy to navigate and a delight to explore—an ideal vacation destination for the single woman.

—→ ARRIVAL

Arriving from North America by plane will involve a connection, probably at Heathrow Airport, then a brief flight to Edinburgh Airport, which is eight miles northwest of the city. The city center can be reached by taxi for around £25 (US $50), or by the number 100 Lothario Airlink Bus for only £4 (US $8); this bus runs every ten to fifteen minutes and stops centrally at Waverley Bridge, where numerous taxis await. Trains also arrive at Waverley Station. National Express buses operate from London to Edinburgh, but the journey will take over ten hours.

→ ACCOMMODATIONS

Edinburgh is not as expensive as many other European cities, and is a lot more reasonable than London, and the number of hotel rooms has increased to match demand over the last few years. Remember, key events cause rooms to be at a premium. August and early September are really, really busy because of the Edinburgh Fringe Festival, Edinburgh International Festival, and Edinburgh Military Tattoo, all of which take place right in the center of the city (www.edinburghfestivals.co.uk). It's a wonderful time to be in the city, with such a colorful array of activities, so book in advance—up to a year in advance is advisable—if you plan to be there then. The most full-of-character accommodations are found in the Old Town, which places the visitor right in the center of things. Some of the larger chain hotels offer deals, especially in the low season of October to April (though not at Christmas and New Year). Check out www.ibishotel.com and www.premiertravelinn.co.uk. There are also quite a few designer hotels springing up; good bed and breakfast offerings can also be had. Accommodations in the New Town are closer to the main shopping area. Remember, some of the older (cheaper) residences may not be that luxurious compared to North American standards; Edinburgh can get very cold, even during the height of summer, so read online reviews to ensure that accommodations are heated.

→ ACTIVITIES

Edinburgh is a wonderful size and can be seen in three days. It can also serve as a base from which to explore other notable Scottish towns and cities, such as Glasgow, Stirling, and Saint Andrews. Spend a week in Edinburgh, and for the first three days get to know the city. On the first day, visit the typical tourist sites in the Old Town (the Royal Mile, Edinburgh Castle, National Gallery). Explore New Town on the second day (Princess Street, including the gardens, and the National Portrait Gallery; shop along Princess Street at the end of the day, and meander along side streets to explore a great selection of secondhand book stores); on the third day, see the Scottish Parliament and Holyrood House, and hike the forty-five minutes up to Arthur's Seat. After three days in Edinburgh, board the train to Glasgow and spend a day there—it's an easy journey that takes under an hour. There is just as much to see in Glasgow as in Edinburgh, so spending a night in Glasgow is also an option. On another occasion, visit the city of Stirling with its picture-perfect castle perched on a volcanic crag. Less touristy, Stirling is a great size to wander around for a day. Finally, consider a trip to Saint Andrews, situated on the coast; it's famous for the university where Prince William met Kate, and is also known for golf. Train travel is easy and safe and provides the traveler with views of the wonderful Scottish scenery.

───> ADDITIONAL INFORMATION

For the single female traveler, Edinburgh is a safe, culturally rich destination to explore. The one issue that may not be in your favor, however, is the weather. It can get very, very cold. It can get very, very wet. It can be very, very gloomy, even in the height of summer, so come prepared. While summers are warm, they are rarely hot (again, great for the menopausal among us), and packing a lightweight rain jacket is essential. Although the Scots speak English, it can be heavily accented and difficult to understand. This accent is a lot thicker in Glasgow; I once spent an entire twenty-minute taxi ride across Glasgow saying, "Sorry, excuse me, can you repeat that? Didn't quite get that," to the smiling, chattering cab driver who was oblivious to the grinning, uncomprehending chick in the back seat. Edinburgh has more restaurants per capita than anywhere else in the UK, some of them very upscale. But when in Edinburgh, or any other Scottish town, I prefer to have a pub lunch while warming myself by the open fire and listening to the lilting Scottish accents. There I observe (and eavesdrop on) the fascinating Scottish characters and enjoy the latest Ian Rankin novel, set within the culture I am experiencing.

→ **WEBSITES**
edinburgh.org
thisisedinburgh.com
visitscotland.com

DUBROVNIK

Take Flight for

WALLED CITY
BEACHES
SAFETY

Those who seek paradise on earth should come to Dubrovnik.

—George Bernard Shaw

⟶ **I INCLUDE DUBROVNIK, CROATIA, EVEN** though I've visited it only once, because of the perfect time I had as a single woman. And Dubrovnik *sounds* so much more exotic and exciting than London, Paris, or Amsterdam when you tell others that it's where you're heading. Most North Americans have difficulty finding it on a map—in fact many do not know where Croatia is, let alone the city of Dubrovnik. It is really a welcoming and safe destination. I am also including it as it offers a lovely beach and ocean access *and* historical/cultural alternatives, thereby meeting two of a woman's most basic needs: reading trashy novels while working on a tan one day, then visiting a historic walled city and learning of its history the next—stimulation of the mind, body, and soul. An excursion to Dubrovnik is an indulgence. Although getting to Dubrovnik from North America is not easy, once you're there, a friendly people with a deep respect and courtesy for the single woman will ensure you have a relaxed time. Dubrovnik has not, as yet, been discovered by the hordes of tourists found in other European cities, although you may question this assertion if you find yourself in the town at the same time as three cruise ships.

⟶ ARRIVAL

Dubrovnik's small airport, ZraĐna Luka (also known as Đilipi, after the nearest small town), is a quaint little affair thirteen miles south of the city. Being small has an advantage: you won't have to wait long for your luggage. From here, you can reach the city in about forty-five minutes by taxi (about $40) or by Croatian Airlines Airport Bus ($6). There are no direct flights from North America, which means that travelers coming from there will have to take a connecting flight to Dubrovnik from a European hub such as London, Amsterdam, or Frankfurt and will have a long travel time, but it is so worth it. A number of charter flights operate from these large European cities, so consider a two-center holiday (e.g., London and Dubrovnik).

⟶ ACCOMMODATIONS

Now for my totally biased, personal recommendation: when visiting Dubrovnik, make plans to stay in the wonderful adjacent town of Cavtat, not Dubrovnik itself. About ten miles south of Dubrovnik, Cavtat is about ten minutes by taxi from the airport.

This sleepy waterfront resort town offers a fantastic, relaxed atmosphere. With sea wall walkways and a horseshoe-shaped harbor, this idyllic fishing town has accommodations ranging from a five-hundred-room designer hotel with its own private beach (Hotel Croatia—one of the largest in the country) to small rooms in private homes (known as *sobas*). Again, I highly recommend staying in Cavtat and not Dubrovnik. Dubrovnik has a reputation for being the most expensive location within Croatia, and while it has some wonderful locations, many of these tend to be away from the Old Town core. Numerous bed and breakfasts and rooms are near the Old Town, but be advised: these can be noisy at night. While there is an accommodations "star rating" in Croatia, take this only as a guideline. Breakfast is usually included, and when it's not there are a number of good restaurants and cafés. Prices increase during the peak summer months of June to August, but April, May, and September offer pleasant, warm temperatures with fewer crowds. If staying in Cavtat, you can reach Dubrovnik by boat (a forty-five minute journey, departing hourly, that can get a little rough if the sea is choppy). You can also take a public bus, which is patronized by a nice mix of locals and tourists.

⟶ ACTIVITIES

The walled city of Dubrovnik is stunning. The primary attraction is the one-and-a-quarter-mile walk around the city on the wall itself. Be prepared for some serious ups and downs and go early (or late) to avoid the crowds. When the cruise ships dock, Dubrovnik gets very busy, so the earlier the start the better. These walls also act as a heat trap and can become very hot. Toilets are available as you walk around, and there are opportunities to buy drinks and stop in small cafés. After exploring the walls, spend a couple of days seeing the attractions in the Old Town. Some of the museums leave little to be desired and are more like high school classrooms you pay to enter than European museums. Although these were somewhat disappointing, I did not begrudge the entrance fee and felt that since the city had experienced such devastation in my lifetime, any attempt to rebuild the economy should be supported. Any disappointment in the contents of these museums was made up for by the quality of the architecture. Wandering around the numerous tourist-oriented shops in the Old Town is safe and visually stimulating. Above the town is Mount Srd, an old Napoleon-built fortress, which was instrumental in the defense of Dubrovnik in the 1990s; there you will find a fascinating museum with a lot of photographs and great views. As mentioned earlier, the community of Cavtat is a delight to visit and has a number of easy-to-access trails (a hike to the mausoleum provides a good workout and awesome views), beaches for sunbathing, a small museum, and a center with cafés and bars. Finally, excursions by boat to the unspoiled Elaphite Islands are also popular and can be taken from Dubrovnik, either by guide or Jadrolinija ferries—a great day out.

→ ADDITIONAL INFORMATION

I took the bus into Dubrovnik from Cavtat and missed the stop, so I ended up at the port. In anywhere else in the world, ports are notorious for being unsavory, often sleazy places, and not the place for a single woman. Not so in Dubrovnik. I walked from the port back to the Old Town with not a care in the world. No begging on the street, no unsavory characters, no dark lanes, no mad drivers at every intersection. The crime rate is low in Croatia, and while some of the bars may be a little male-dominated (what's new?), I loved the way I could take the bus, ferry, or taxi, walk the streets in the day and early evening, and feel utterly safe. Croatian currency is the kuna (kn). While English is widely understood, not everyone speaks it, but it's still easy to make yourself understood. Restrooms are easily available in the Old Town, but in other areas can only be found in transportation hubs and restaurants. Dubrovnik is a great location if you want to relax in the sun, visit an ancient culture, and explore safely without a care in the world.

⟶ WEBSITES
croatia.hr
tzdubrovnik.hr
visit-croatia.co.uk/index.php/croatia-destinations/dubrovnik

FURTHER RESOURCES

SUGGESTED PACKING LIST

→ **SUITCASE CONTENTS**

- lightweight rain jacket
- comfortable walking shoes
- other shoes/sandals
- gloves
- jacket/fleece
- jeans/pants
- skirt/dress
- shorts
- T-shirts
- shirts
- rain/sun hat
- scarves
- underwear
- socks
- sweater
- swimsuit
- belt
- sleep shirt/pjs

→ **TOILETRY BAG CONTENTS**

- brush/comb
- toothpaste
- dental floss
- toothbrush
- deodorant/ antiperspirant
- tissues
- makeup
- moisturizer
- cleanser
- toner
- shampoo/conditioner
- body cream
- sewing kit
- nail scissors
- nail polish remover
- tweezers
- feminine hygiene products
- hair accessories
- small mirror

MEDICATION

- Band-Aids
- contact lens solutions
- cotton swabs
- diarrhea medication
- insect repellent
- sting relief
- motion sickness pills
- headache pills/ pain killers
- antiseptic cream
- hormone replacement therapy medication
- vitamin pills
- sunscreen
- any additional medication taken daily

ADDITIONAL ITEMS

- sunglasses
- alarm clock (if not on phone)
- corkscrew
- bottle opener
- plastic cutlery
- earplugs
- electrical converter/ adaption plug/charger
- cell phone/tablet charger
- washing powder
- key-ring flashlight
- pens
- journal
- books
- water bottle
- reusable shopping bags
- telescoping umbrella
- binoculars
- granola bars/instant oatmeal/instant coffee

DOCUMENTS

- passport
- driver's license
- travel insurance
- tickets
- copies of passport
- visas
- business cards

ONLINE INFORMATION

The aim of this book is to encourage women to take flight and see the world. At the outset, I acknowledged there are hundreds of guidebooks, websites, and blogs, as well as a great deal of tourist literature that contain far more comprehensive information than the scanty suggestions given in this book. Anyone planning a vacation should visit the city's tourist information website (listed for each city I include). Additional resources can be found at the following sites:

→ **TRAVEL LITERATURE—BOOKS AND WEBSITES**

Blue Guides (blueguides.com)
Eyewitness Travel (dk.com)
Fodor's (fodors.com)
Frommer's Guides (frommers.com)
Insight Travel Guides—Berlitz (insightguides.com)
Let's Go (letsgo.com)
Lonely Planet (lonelyplanet.com)
Moon Travel Guides (moon.com)
National Geographic (nationalgeographic.com)
Rick Steves (ricksteves.com)
Rough Guides (roughguides.com)
Time Out Guides (timeout.com)

→ **TRAVEL PLANNING WEBSITES**

booking.com
expedia.com
hotels.com
kayak.com
orbitz.com
travelocity.com
tripadvisor.com
trivago.com

→ **WEBSITES SPECIFICALLY FOR WOMEN TRAVELERS**

aa.com/women
adventurewomen.com
gutsytraveler.com
journeywoman.com
TodaysWomanTraveller.com
women-traveling.com
womenstravelnetwork.ca
womentraveltips.com

→ **HEALTH-RELATED WEBSITES**

cdc.gov
fco.gov.uk
iamet.org
phac-aspc.gc.ca
tripprep.com
who.int

→ **GOVERNMENT-RELATED WEBSITES**

aaa.com/vacation/idpf.html
caa.ca/travelling/idp/
fco.gov.uk
travel.state.gov

→ **CURRENCY EXCHANGE RATE WEBSITES**

xe.com
x-rates.com

OTHER USEFUL WEBSITES

mapquest.com
theweathernetwork.com
timeanddate.com
visaconnection.com
weather.com
weatherbase.com
worldtimezone.com

ACKNOWLEDGMENTS

As any writer knows, it is not enough to have a fantastic idea for a book, or a completed word-perfect manuscript—the real difficulty is in persuading a publisher to share your conviction that the subject is worthy of all the time (and money) necessary to turn that manuscript into a bestseller. It is a huge gamble. In this respect, my first debt of gratitude goes to the team at TouchWood Editions—Taryn Boyd, Pat Touchie, Tori Elliot, and Renée Layberry—for believing in me and in *Time to Take Flight*. Without them, this idea may have remained just that—an idea.

In many respects, *Time to Take Flight* is autobiographical; it has been inspired and structured by the women who have been instrumental in shaping and guiding me over the years. I love my female friends and yet rarely reflect on their profound influence on my development as a person and as a confident solo traveler. My high school girlfriends—Janine Crawford, Julie Boak, Jacqui Newman, and Claire Worrall—were there for me (through their much-needed letters of support and news from home) when I traveled by myself for the first time in the late 1970s. And they were there for me when I got back. No matter where I go and for how long, when we reconnect they greet me with the same level of affection. They comprise the foundation of my female friendships and I am lucky to know them.

The women I met through my academic career taught me how to live by myself and steered my understanding of the benefits of travel through the vehicle of study. In different cities and countries, Sally Dent, Alexandra Seaton, Kathleen

Burke, and Susan Boyd acted as sounding boards for my eclectic passions, providing voices of reason, humor, and support, but always tolerating my idiosyncrasies. I cherish knowing them.

The mothers I came to know through my children—Grainne Hoy, Gillian Beath, Lorraine White-Wilkinson, and Diana Robertson—have watched me grow (and age) as together we navigated the difficult task of child (and husband) rearing and teenager tolerance; they were always just a phone call away should I need anything. I'm also grateful to the twenty or so women who regularly exercise at the Kerrisdale Community Centre in Vancouver and whom I see on an almost-daily basis. Over the years this diverse group of fit babes, ranging in age from twenty-five to seventy-five, have provided countless hours of counseling and advice on such issues as my rapidly aging menopausal body, teenage angst, Spanx underwear, the merits of karaoke, the application of lipstick, and, of course, travel. Unbeknownst to them, they have informed the many ideas and topics in this work. Some of these women also took the time to read and comment on earlier drafts of the manuscript. They each add a perfect grounding to my work life—a grounding that I hope never to be without.

Finally, I want to thank the woman who generously and consistently told me to take flight: my mother. I owe her the most of all.

JAYNE SEAGRAVE was born in England and moved to Canada in 1991. She lives in Vancouver with her husband, Andrew, and two teenage sons, Jack and Sam. She has a PHD in criminology and is the best-selling author of eight books covering topics such as policing, business, and camping. She is currently researching and writing a book detailing the story of the internationally acclaimed Shakespearean theater company Bard on the Beach. For the last twenty years she has been the marketing director for the Vancouver Tool Corporation (www.vancouvertool.com), which she owns with her partner. This position, coupled with an inherent love of learning about other cultures and countries and an unbridled passion for travel—locally and internationally— led to the creation of *Time to Take Flight*.